The Whitewater Wars

By David Brown

Adventures on the Gorge photo

The Rafters and the River Trip
that Saved the Ocoee
&
The Battle for the Gauley River

Copyright © 2020 David Brown

All rights reserved. No part of this publication may be reproduced, distributed, or transmitted in any form or by any means, including photocopying, recording, or other electronic or mechanical methods, without the prior written permission of the publisher, except in the case of brief quotations embodied in critical reviews and certain other noncommercial uses permitted by copyright law. For permission requests, write to the publisher, addressed to the address below.

David Brown
P.O. Box 66
Strawberry Plains, TN 37871

Dedication

This book is a story about the men and women who without money or experience successfully battled federal agencies to save two classic whitewater rivers and their recreational experiences. This book is dedicated to all those mentioned and unmentioned who contributed to those efforts. And to my wife Robin who stuck by me all these years and to my daughter Hillary who gave me a reason to endure so many challenges.

Acknowledgements

A special thanks to Marc Hunt and David Arnold who helped review the text for accuracy and for their additions to the story and to Hilary Wickes for editing assistance. Thanks to Gary Harper for use of his original photos from the Ocoee days, to Adventures on the Gorge, and to Terry Ritterbush, Whitewater Photography, Fayetteville, WV for many photos used in the Gauley story.

Cover photos: Ocoee River photo Sunburst Adventures. Gauley River photo Adventures on the Gorge

The Rafters and the River Trip that Saved the Ocoee River

In the Beginning

Trouble was brewing. As I deposited my meager life savings in the Bank of Benton in Ocoee, Tennessee, the bank teller looked down at me with a frown. "We don't like outsiders moving in here," she said as she handed me a receipt. It was September 1980, and my red beard was a dead give-away that another whitewater hippie was moving in to paddle the rapids of the Ocoee River. A Washington state tag still adorned my back bumper which confirmed her suspicions. Little did she know, I had a slightly higher standing than "outsider" and it was about to throw the county into turmoil.

The Ocoee River courses through Polk County, Tennessee, an all but forgotten crossroads in the southeastern corner of the state. With only 13,600 residents in 1980 over 60% of the county's land was taken up by the Cherokee National Forest. The South was just beginning its economic expansion, but growth and change had taken a detour around Polk County. There were no African American residents in the county in 1980. Not one fast food franchise. A small group kept a tight grip on political power and resisted outsiders. Living there as a disciple of the emerging whitewater industry was living on the edge.

In the Beginning

I moved into the county after a band of outfitters led by Marc Hunt had cobbled together enough money to hire me to be the Executive Director of the fledgling Ocoee River Council (ORC) for the handsome sum of $150 per week. Our goal was to save the whitewater rapids of the Ocoee River from the Tennessee Valley Authority's plan to rebuild the Ocoee No. 2 hydroelectric project and divert water around the riverbed. The project consisted of a diversion dam, a 4.5-mile-long wooden flume line and a powerhouse. The wooden flume line was one of the two working hydropower flume lines still in use when it was shut down in 1976.

The Ocoee River Council could just as well have been named "let's do something even if it's wrong," because we were clueless. No one gave us a chance of winning the battle against the all-powerful Tennessee Valley Authority, the nation's largest public utility. But we were driven and that meant trouble for TVA.

Arriving in Polk County in the late summer, I described my unemployment as a sabbatical, a pretentious description which lost its luster when I had to admit I was living out of my car. My beard, frayed wardrobe and wildly runner's physique rendered me unemployable by most businesses wary of hippie-types. I was not a hippie but had fallen irretrievably into the outdoor lifestyle where shaving was not a priority. It had probably even cost me my chance to attend graduate school in marketing and advertising despite having the appropriate grade point average.

THE WHITEWATER WARS

After living in and around wilderness for 18 months, my soul ached for some purpose in life. Five years earlier I had helped start a cardiac rehabilitation program at the behest of a renowned cardiologist. The program was a great success, but I sacrificed it and a future as a bureaucrat in the Veterans Administration to follow my heart into the outdoors. Wilderness canoeing in Canada and a 400-mile canoe trip to the Arctic Ocean on the Coppermine River sealed my fate. In 1979 I hit the road with most of my possessions in the back of my station wagon, headed to Washington state where I took up residence until I could figure out what to do next.

Mount Stewart in eastern Washington beckoned in May 1980. News reports indicated an eruption of Mt. Saint Helens was inevitable and more likely when the sun and moon aligned to tug on the magma. I convinced my friends to drag me up the slopes that weekend. It was May 18, 1980 when the volcano blew killing 57 people. Three of us watched the eruption from the south slope of Stewart. I was not a competent climber, but my friends were, and they knew the best route to view the event if it happened.

My plan had been to relocate to Washington but there were no decent jobs at the height of the recession in 1980, prompting me to reconsider the move. A road sign in Seattle purportedly asked the last person to leave to turn out the lights. The St. Helens eruption and the ash fall, which scurried about on the wind like a permanent snow, confirmed my plans to head back to the southeast for post-graduate studies.

In the Beginning

During those studies I ventured back to the Ocoee to paddle, noticing that the Ocoee power project construction was getting underway. The challenge to save the Ocoee captured my interest. Eventually, I asked Bill Miller, President of the Tennessee Valley Canoe Club, to help me find out what was going on.

Ocoee paddlers, 1978.

Late that summer, I took up residence in my car at a Forest Service campground near the Ocoee, leaving more possessions at a neighbor's house, which I never retrieved. During this sojourn, my girlfriend had capriciously dumped me for a nuclear engineer with a six-figure salary. In later years, a stock joke in the whitewater industry was that homelessness was defined as a raft guide who had just lost his girlfriend. That was me, though I had yet to guide a raft. Only the emerging whitewater industry of 1980, inhabited by young unaffected entrepreneurs, would have chosen me to lead the battle to save a premier recreation asset from the nation's largest utility.

I met Marc Hunt, co-owner of Sunburst, on the gravel bar next to Double Trouble rapid earlier that summer and began promoting a broader effort to save the river. Later, he invited me to come down from my automobile residence on Chilhowee Mountain to live in his guide house while he and his colleagues figured out what to do about the Ocoee situation. We planned an Ocoee Day for publicity in early September with paddling clubs, hosting a couple of politicians on the river, who without realizing the extent of their political peril, made supportive statements about the river. One of the politicians later told me that TVA had put their union colleagues on him after his appearance.

During the event, Marc asked me to climb onto the back of a raft trailer to address the small crowd gathered in the parking lot. We were amazed when the press flooded the event, which despite our lack of press releases, generated enormous publicity. Libby Wann, a writer for the Chattanooga Times, wrote a big feature about the history of the flume line. She was clearly in the tank for TVA, but the media attention helped congeal support for our efforts among outfitters and paddlers.

In the Beginning

Many Ocoee outfitters were still trying to decide if this rafting business they had fallen into was worth a fight. Slowly we began to generate interest among other outfitters which led to the Ocoee Day success. Afterwards, Marc and Dick Eustis, Ocoee manager for the vaunted Nantahala Outdoor Center, organized a van tour to talk with groups who had tangled with the agency. We met with TVA Chairman David Freeman, who was supportive but let us know others in the agency were not. While Freeman supported recreation on the river, TVA's Office of Power in Chattanooga, led by Hugh Parris, would hear none of it, and the Office of Power was calling the shots.

At the end of the last leg of our van tour, the crew pulled into a Cracker Barrell to take a leak. I told them if they did not get their act together, I was moving back to Washington state. Bill Miller had already proposed the Ocoee River Council made up of paddlers and private boaters, but it had to be funded. Marc and Dick emerged from the Cracker Barrell to offer me the $ 150/week job – about the same that rank-and-file raft guides earned at the time. I accepted on the spot. It was a gift I would never forget and unbeknownst to me at the time, initiated a 40-year-long career in the whitewater and outfitting industry.

By 1980 the Ocoee River was rapidly becoming the centerpiece for whitewater recreation in the southern United States. It was accessible to large population centers and sported constant whitewater rapids, which were relatively benign compared to other whitewater runs of similar status. We knew the Ocoee was worth the fight, but we had no idea just how right we were. It would eventually become the most popular whitewater river in America, host the 1996 Olympic whitewater canoe and kayak event, and see over 7 million visitors over the next 35 years.

None of that potential seemed to matter to TVA. Use of the river for whitewater recreation was a threat to the agency's Office of Power, which had no interest in having the benefits of its power project sliced off by a bunch of paddlers in river shorts and sandals. They thought they could flip us away like a dandruff flake.

As river enthusiasts, we had to pivot from simply opposing power projects and dams to demonstrating the economic benefits of recreation to get some of the water stored by the projects for recreational use. It would be a lesson that propelled whitewater recreation in the eastern U.S. for years to come. Unlike western rivers with snowpack for water storage, by midsummer many eastern whitewater runs were dependent on water releases from upstream dams to provide flows attractive to whitewater rafting customers and paddlers. To be of value and to enable reservations for raft trips, those releases had to be on a reliable schedule. At that time kayakers and canoeists, also known as private boaters, had no chance of getting extensive water releases in competition with hydropower. It took the economic benefits provided by commercial rafting to compete and that meant a lot of raft customers who also provided a much larger political constituency. We had to overcome the mantra that 'power is always better than recreation'. On the Ocoee, recreation would eventually have more value than the minor amount of power lost when TVA provided water releases. But getting the public and politicians to understand that would be an enormous challenge.

The Tennessee Valley Authority's Kingdom

For years, the Tennessee Valley Authority's reign over the Valley had been unquestioned. By 1980, a series of management missteps began to unfold just as the Ocoee controversy emerged. Those travails created a political liability and provided an opening for the Ocoee River Council.

In the nineteen sixties TVA's three-member board of directors launched an ambitious plan to construct 17 nuclear reactors. The agency already enjoyed a surplus of generating capacity and failed to account for the growth in generation capacity by other utilities. By 1980, nuclear projects under construction were already running into management and technical problems. The engineering skills and care required to build nuclear power plants were different from those required to build dams and coal-fired power plants. Many of the reactors would eventually be cancelled, costing the agency billions of dollars, and creating a mountain of debt. The four-reactor Bellefonte nuclear power plant in (ironically) Hollywood, Alabama would eventually become the nation's richest investment in an uncompleted construction project. TVA spent over $5 billion on the project before it was finally cancelled.

Following the same bureaucratic instincts to plow ahead regardless of the costs, TVA got the antique Ocoee No. 2 hydroelectric project and its 4.5-mile wooden flume line listed on the National Register of Historic Places to ensure that it would be rebuilt and maintained to 1913 specifications.

Created in 1933 during the Great Depression by Franklin D. Roosevelt to provide flood control and economic development to the rural Tennessee River Valley, TVA had been protected by the Valley's congressional delegation for years. Its congressionally authorized, autonomous corporate structure as a quasi-federal agency and its historic benefits to the Tennessee Valley economy made TVA sacrosanct. At its peak, TVA boasted over 50,000 employees and contractors. Many residents of the Valley still equated TVA's electrification of the region with the economic renaissance that led it out of the Great Depression.

The Tellico Dam controversy emerged in the late 1970's just as rivers were growing in popularity as weekend playgrounds for baby boomers. Today, its shimmering reservoir at the foot of Appalachian Mountains is another jewel in the strand of reservoirs holding back the headwaters of the Tennessee River. By 1980 the Tellico Dam controversy had eroded TVA's hallowed status among baby boomers. TVA's strong-arm tactics against landowners gave momentum to ORC's efforts on the Ocoee and damaged the agency's credibility, particularly among newspaper reporters.

THE WHITEWATER WARS

In the late 1960's, TVA was still a dam-building agency at heart, despite running out of locations for purposeful projects. In 1936 TVA listed 69 potential dam sites in the Tennessee River Valley. TVA would build 60. To facilitate dam construction, Congress had given TVA unlimited powers of eminent domain to confiscate private property from poor rural farmers and resell the land to whomever it saw fit. "Wild River", a 1960 movie starring Montgomery Cliff and Lee Remick, relived the struggles landowners faced as TVA began building dams throughout the valley. The Tellico Dam would be the final TVA dam constructed on the last stretch of what had been the Little Tennessee River.

Tellico Dam. Photo from Tennessee Valley Authority.

The battle for the last remnant of the "Little T" was a classic conservation battle that created an environment for favorable media coverage of the Council's Ocoee campaign. The "Little T" was a remnant of a once magnificent 200-million-year-old, 135-mile mountain river. The seeps and springs dripping from the moss-covered rocks of the Great Smoky Mountains gave birth to the "Little T" before it turned toward the Tennessee Valley, creating cascades and drops that would become sites for dams.

The Little T's headwaters were inhabited by native brook trout and its lower reaches by the snail darter, a little fish about the size of a big paper clip. Rainbow and brown trout stocked below the dams in the Little T created a trout fishery for fly fishermen. Allied with a handful of zealous lawyers and trout fishermen, the snail darter would stop a huge federal bureaucracy dead in its tracks, temporarily. The accomplished lawyers who fished for the Little T's trout were among those who made up the "Tellico Dam resisters," although some worked in the background to avoid the rough hand of TVA which dominated the political culture from its headquarters in Knoxville.

The irony of this legal battle was that some of the plaintiffs who used the snail darter and the Endangered Species Act to stop the Tellico Dam project were really interested in preserving the trout fishery sustained by stocking nonnative rainbow and brown trout below the dams. Still this last remnant of the Little T was well worth the battle to river lovers.

Zygmunt Plater, a University of Tennessee law professor, emerged as the lead attorney in the legal battle to save the Little T. Plater's book, <u>The Snail Darter and the Dam</u> recounts the twists and turn of the battle to save the Little T. The story of that battle was really not the snail darter, but about saving a river valley and the confiscation of private land for a purely discretionary project by an agency with unbridled powers of eminent domain.

In 1973, the plight of the Little T was brought to the attention of Plater by a law student, Hank Hill. Hill was an associate of Dr. David Etnier, who, reports say, discovered the snail darter while scuba diving in the Little T. Hill, Plater, and a few Knoxville attorneys were among those who successfully petitioned the U.S. Fish and Wildlife Service to put the snail darter on the Endangered Species List. The Little T was designated critical habitat. A subsequent lawsuit wound its way to the Supreme Court, which upheld a 6th Circuit Court's injunction halting completion of the Tellico Dam project. The Justices ruled that the Endangered Species Act was inviolate – there could be no exception to it regardless of the money already sunk into the project. But TVA flexed its political muscle. In 1979 Congress exempted the Tellico project from the Endangered Species Act allowing the Tellico Dam's reservoir to be filled, revealing the dangers of unbridled federal agency power and its tentacles embedded deep in the political fabric of a financially dependent community

Mysteriously, during planning for the Tellico project, TVA set about acquiring far more land than it needed to build the dam and reservoir. Justifications for the project shifted after it was envisioned in the late 1930's. No power would ever be generated by the Tellico dam, and its flood control benefits were minimal. It was a dam in search of a purpose. In 1959 TVA's infamous chairman Aubrey "Red" Wagner latched onto land development as its purpose and dedicated himself to the dam's completion, running over anyone who stood in his way.

Beryl Moser was among those flattened by TVA's steamroller and displaced by the Tellico Dam's reservoir. TVA paid $12,800 for his five acres of land. Moser was among the last holdouts until broken by the strong arm of a federal agency and the federal marshals who forced him off his land just before the reservoir was filled. According to a report in the Knoxville News Sentinel, one half-acre of his property was inundated by the reservoir. The rest, which was not covered by the Tellico reservoir, would ultimately be resold for $300,000 an acre, according to the News Sentinel report. Today, the land around the Little T, once owned by rural farmers, is home to golf course communities and boat manufacturing plants. These events would be described as crony capitalism today, aided in the 1970's, by politicians from both political parties.

Reporters from United Press International (UPI) were among those disaffected by TVA's strong-arm tactics during Tellico Dam fight. The story of an elderly woman, who was pulled from her house by marshals after which the house was flattened by bulldozers, still rung in the ears of many. Her only desire had been to live out her days on her 100-acre farm. The same UPI reporters covering the Tellico Dam controversy would also report extensively on the Ocoee battle and the travails that plagued reconstruction of its wooden flume line. They helped generate state-wide and national coverage for the Ocoee.

I was new to the Valley and really did not have an axe to grind with TVA. But many fighting for the Ocoee were influenced by the power wielded by TVA during the Tellico Dam battle. J.T. Lemons, one of the first Ocoee outfitters, and I met with Hank Hill, the law student from the Little T battle, one Saturday morning near Chattanooga to hear him recite the challenges of fighting TVA.

The lesson learned from the fight to save the Little T was simple: political power trumps legal challenges. The Ocoee River Council decided to focus on building political support. But we pushed all the buttons, including using a legal challenge in 1981 in a partially successful attempt to win reconsideration for recreational water releases. While we would eventually lose the lawsuit, it gave ORC stature and heightened media awareness.

The Ocoee No. 2 Flume Line

The Ocoee No. 2 project had originally been completed in 1913. Its wooden flume line, which carried the river's entire flow during normal run-off was built on a five-mile long bench carved out of the gorge adjacent to the river by Eastern Tennessee Power Company. The project provided electricity to nearby Chattanooga at the dawn of the Tennessee Valley's electrification. There was no significant reservoir behind the old wooden diversion dam that forced the Ocoee's waters from the riverbed into the flume line. The wooden "stick dam", as it was known to locals, seems feeble by today's standards but its ingenious crib construction withstood the ravages of nature for over 60 years.

The original Ocoee No. 2 stick dam built around 1913 was still intact in 1976. Gary Harper Photo

THE WHITEWATER WARS

Icicles hanging from the old leaky flume line. Gary Harper photo

From 1912 to 1943, flume line workers lived in Caney Creek Village, constructed just for them on the banks of the river downstream of the Ocoee No. 2 powerhouse. In the early 20th century a fully electrified village in the backwoods of Tennessee was highly unusual. According to an historical account of village life by author Debbie Moore, "Caney Creek Village had a hotel, trolley, one room schoolhouse, telephones, concrete sidewalks, electricity, and indoor plumbing." When TVA took control of the property in 1939, the village was vacated. According to Moore's account, TVA revived Caney Creek Village for a short time during the construction of Ocoee Dam #3 during World War II. Today, only concrete foundations remain.

While the Ocoee No. 2 project was an important power source in the first part of the 20th Century, it had minimal value as a power project by 1976, when leaks and disrepair required TVA to take it out of service, allowing water to return to the riverbed. In winter months, great icicles caused by leaks hung from the flume. As plans to rebuild the project got underway, TVA acknowledged in their Environmental Impact Statement that the project's entire annual benefits would not be noticeable in power rates. The project plate capacity, the maximum amount of power it could generate, was only about 21 megawatts. That represented just $7/10,000^{ths}$ of TVA's generating capacity at the time.

Polk County's Welcome Wagon

The nightmare for TVA's Ocoee project employees and their allies in Polk County began when whitewater enthusiasts discovered the lure of Ocoee whitewater when the flume was shut down on Labor Day weekend 1976. Marc Hunt and his future business partner Bill Chipley were driving east in the early morning light along Highway 64 toward the nearby Chattooga River, when they saw rapids in the Ocoee's previously dry riverbed. They quickly diverted their paddling expedition to the Ocoee. During that run and other excursions in early September, the seeds were planted for Sunburst, one of the river's first whitewater rafting companies, which opened the next spring.

The growth of whitewater recreation was in its heyday. Paddlers and kayakers, known to locals as "the rafters", began riding the rapids. Marc and Bill, J.T. Lemons and his three partners, Gary Harper, James Torrence, and Bob Baker were among the pioneering rafting outfitters to run commercial river trips in 1977. They gave many of the rapids their classic names from the paddler's lexicon: Broken Nose, Slice 'n Dice, Double Trouble, Table Saw, and Hell Hole.

The reborn river was four and one-half miles of thrilling Class III – IV whitewater. In those days, the rafting

Polk County's Welcome Wagon

An early Sunburst poster circa 1978. Sunburst, one of the original Ocoee rafting companies founded by Marc Hunt and Bill Chipley, is no longer in business.

experience sold itself. Seven thousand people rafted the river in 1977. By 1980, the number of rafters had grown to fifty-six thousand.

In 1979, Governor Lamar Alexander filmed a commercial for the Tennessee Department of Tourism with Jerry Reed, the country music singer and occasional movie star. The broadcast of their infectiously joyous journey through "Hell Hole" rapid opened the flood gates. Rafters and paddlers flocked to the river. Despite the river's growing popularity, there was no campaign in place to save it.

During the planning of the Ocoee No. 2 project, which began with scoping around 1977, TVA's statements led most outfitters and paddlers to believe the agency was

THE WHITEWATER WARS

Gary and Beth Harper, guiding a raft through Double Trouble. 1978.

going to provide water releases after completion of the project. The original environmental impact statement for the Ocoee No. 2 project was published in 1978. TVA proposed an alternative that would provide for 84 days of recreation. For that reason, there was no outright opposition to the project's reconstruction. But when the project was authorized by the TVA board, they dropped a bomb. Water releases would be contingent on reimbursement for the power TVA lost when water was returned to the riverbed. The cost to provide water releases for 84 days of rafting would be $5 million. Later an engineer who reviewed TVA's calculation said the agency used the highest possible projections of coal costs to justify their bill for lost power.

Polk County's Welcome Wagon

Like many eastern whitewater runs, the Ocoee was a natural river, but its reliable water flows were a creation of TVA's hydroelectric power generation just upstream of the popular stretch of whitewater. The Ocoee battle was not a fight against the project itself but an effort to make some reasonable adjustment to include recreation as a project benefit, something that TVA was not prepared to do.

TVA's Ocoee No. 2 employees were threatened by the migration of "outsiders" to the county. The invasion of paddlers, some of whom even established residence there, was a culture shock for some of the locals in this remote corner of Tennessee. During a public scoping session, as project reconstruction was being planned, one local said he did not mind the whitewater but resented the "nudeness" along the river while he was driving his family to church on Sunday morning. Kayakers were not nudist; they simply had no place to change clothes before paddling the river.

Then there was the County's welcome wagon for paddlers run by Sheriff "Whitey" Ramsey that turned tourism into a profit center for local law enforcement. Polk County had this arcane ordinance that made it illegal to have an open container of alcohol in public. Few tourists were aware of the law. On weekend nights the Sheriff's Department, with the acquiescence of the Forest Service, ran stakeouts in the Forest Service campgrounds arresting anyone drinking a beer in public. Marc had a group of 20 no-shows for a raft trip one Saturday. The group from Atlanta had been arrested the night prior and taken to jail. Marc successfully pled with the jailer to let them out so the raft trip could go on.

Whitey was not to be trifled with and did not always take prisoners. Marc remembers the day Whitey got word that a local bank was being robbed. Whitey set up across from the bank with his rifle and shot the robber dead as he exited the bank. As Jimmy Buffet would say, "no picture on a poster, no reward and no bail".

The Battle Lines Are Drawn

Don Curbow, the manager of TVA's Ocoee projects led the not-so-merry band of TVA employees who opposed recreation on the Ocoee River. Federal employees are not supposed to lobby, but he lobbied and more. The ineptitude of their efforts was almost comical except that some crossed the line. In the early days of the battle, Curbow and his band roamed the County when inspired to action, appearing at political events and the occasional hearing. One night in the winter of 1981 they descended on Johnny Thomasson at his Cherokee Corners gas station. Johnny was the only native Polk County resident running an outfitting business on the Ocoee in 1981. I arrived at the Cherokee Corners station that night for a snack to find Curbow and his crew arguing with Johnny. Realizing I was intruding on an ugly exchange, I backed toward the door. Curbow followed. "You're ruining this county," Curbow spat, as he pushed me out the door.

We were made aware of Mr. Curbow's opposition to recreation on the river in the early fall of 1980 at a townhall meeting in a school auditorium in the Copper Basin. Although it was a longshot, at the time we were still hopeful for a Congressional appropriation to cover water releases. We were not opposing rehabilitation of the flume line. Our biggest problem politically, was that TVA's Office of Power was headquartered in Chattanooga, the hometown of Congresswoman Marilyn Lloyd Bouquard, whose support was critical to a legislative solution. But she was far more sensitive to the interests of TVA than an upstart group of whitewater enthusiasts and outfitters.

At the townhall, State Senator Ben Longley made an opening statement, which supported both recreation and completion of the flume line. But it was an odd performance – almost like he did not want to be there. Mr. Curbow followed with a statement that was hostile to the continuation of whitewater recreation on the river. He told the group of about 50 people that releasing water into the riverbed would cost ratepayers $5,000 per day. After I complained to Tish Jenkins, TVA's Southeastern District Administrator, that Mr. Curbow was lobbying against recreation on the river, she summoned me to her office a couple of weeks later to give a deposition to one of the agency attorneys. I never figured out what that was about.

Shortly after the townhall, another TVA Ocoee project employee undermined our political standing when he criticized Ocoee outfitters at a Cleveland City Commission meeting, as reported by the Cleveland Daily Banner. He asserted that Ocoee outfitters were not local residents but lived in North Carolina, Chattanooga and Atlanta. He claimed that local citizens would lose their jobs if the project was not completed. He asked the Commission to pass a resolution supporting completion

The Battle Lines Are Drawn

of the project, which also provided for the continuation of recreation on the river. But his message to the Commission was that we were not residents of the area, which undermined our political standing.

The start of the Ocoee No. 2 project's reconstruction coincided with the creation of the Ocoee River Council in the fall of 1980. The ORC had no better ally in its effort to gain attention for their battle than TVA's own employees at the Ocoee projects, who would not shrink from the defense of their cherished flume line with its roots embedded in Polk County's history and culture. Soon after ORC's formation, a petition opposing recreation on the Ocoee showed up at Laddy's Gulf, a busy gas station on U.S. Highway 64, across from the Ocoee No. 2 construction headquarters. Laddy's was known for its grease spot in the pavement out front and Laddy himself - cheerful owner with a strong southern Appalachian accent. When I heard about the petition, I went to the station to read and examine it. There were about 80 signed names on it at that time.

To say that some of TVA's Ocoee project employees had a contempt for "the rafters" was an understatement. Cat Potts, Marc's girlfriend, once called the Ocoee No. 2 powerhouse for information about water flows, only to be asked what color panties she was wearing.

If not for the Ocoee's whitewater, the 40-square mile Copper Basin, denuded by open-pit copper smelting, would have been the County's top landmark. In 1980 the bare red clay hills still stuck out like a sore thumb,

THE WHITEWATER WARS

TVA rushed to get the Ocoee No. 2 project construction underway in 1980. Gary Harper photo.

visible from earth's orbit. Copper had been discovered by European settlers in the Basin in 1843. As the story goes, smelting technology of the day was "chop wood, pile up, dump ore, light fire." The smoke often mixed with fog and mist to create sulfuric acid clouds over the basin which rained back down on the slopes partially exposed by the wood harvesting used for smelting

The Battle Lines Are Drawn

bonfires. By the early twentieth century, everything green had passed-away or been cut for firewood. In 1980 there was a modern industrial mine and a smelting operation, but it was playing out. The Basin still retained the environmental scars from the early years of mining.

By 1980 change, not sulfuric acid, was in the air. TVA's Ocoee project employees regarded that change as more corrosive to their culture than H2SO4. They were not going to stand by idly as "the rafters" took over the County.

In October of that year I began my $150 per week job as Director of the Ocoee River Council (ORC) with vigor if not direction, armed with a cranky manual typewriter that had to be as old as TVA's flume line. There was no correction key for the typewriter or our nascent efforts. TVA was a $4 billion-dollar federal agency. ORC's budget barely broke $10,000 in 1981. Fortunately for us, the Ocoee whitewater experience was accessible, powerful, and inspiring beyond description. The number of rafters and kayakers visiting the river through its motley band of outfitters slowly but surely created a viable political constituency. During our campaign, Governor Lamar Alexander received more mail in support of Ocoee whitewater than any other issue as the whitewater community in the southeast rallied around ORC and the river.

Meanwhile, the petition asking Congress to forever bar the rafters from the Ocoee River (and Polk County) and to oppose the appropriation to pay for water releases had garnered about 200 real signatures before it disappeared from the counter at Laddy's Gulf station. It had been forgotten until Tish Jenkins; TVA's Southeastern District Administrator's call came in one December morning in 1980. She said Congress had received a petition against recreation on the Ocoee with more than 2,000 names on it. My heart sunk at the news of this political catastrophe. But something Ms. Jenkins said was curious. She said I should come to her office to look at the petition.

I could barely stay on the road driving to her office a few miles away in Cleveland, Tennessee. A quick scan of the list revealed Jake Kerr's name. Jake was a friend who rented a building to Marc, owner of Sunburst, one of the rafting companies. Ms. Jenkins gave me a copy of the petition which I took to Jake.

"David, there are dead people on this petition," Jake shouted upon review. His face flushed with anger. Before I uttered a word of caution, Jake jumped in his car headed to the Cleveland newspaper.

I was nervous. There had already been some threatening situations. Two burly guys in a pickup had shown up at the house late one night. I had pulled in behind them while they were waiting up the driveway, jotting down their tag number. After I turned around, they left without incident. I thought it was Curbow just paying a visit. But I had to wonder if my situation was about to get worse.

The petition and its forged names made big news throughout the state. The Cleveland Daily Banner ran a front-page story a few days later: "TVA Petition Involvement Investigated". TVA's investigation probably started soon after reporters called to inquire about the petition. Jake, who had once worked on the flume line, was active in County politics, later told me that someone had taken old school bond petitions, cut the top off and copied the names to the statement against recreation on the river. He had signed school bond petitions, but not the petition against rafting. Over 2,000 names had been affixed to the petition against recreation on the Ocoee. It was the same one I read at Laddy's station. The Cleveland Daily Banner investigated the signatures and found that in addition to Jake's signature others said they never signed the petition against recreation on the river. Jake claimed the original petition was circulated by an Ocoee project employee and must have told Cleveland Daily Banner reporter that. According to media reports, someone within TVA had also questioned the legitimacy of the signatures. I never knew how the TVA investigation into their employees' involvement began unless it came from one of these two sources.

Cleveland Daily Banner, Cleveland, Tennessee, December 7, 1980. In the article I appeal to TVA to make the Ocoee No. 2 a multiple purpose project and provide for recreational releases.

After the first of the year Ms. Jenkins called a meeting in her office with others involved with tourism in the region to give reports on their progress. After it adjourned, I hung back until the room had cleared and asked Ms. Jenkins about the status of the TVA investigation into the petition. She blurted out, "They are mad as hell at Curbow!", referring to the investigation. Her response left me with the opinion that TVA knew or had strong suspicions there was employee involvement in the petition.

When TVA announced the results of their investigation into employee involvement a few weeks later, they denied there had been any employee involvement and subtly implied that we set them up. I was incensed. At least the investigation shutdown the political activity of Ocoee project employees in opposition to recreation subsided and we co-existed while the issue played out over the next two and a half years.

But the petition debacle made it clear to me that we could not trust the leadership of TVA to accept recreation on the river. On April 15, 1981 the Ocoee River Council, David Broemel and Sunburst Adventures filed a lawsuit in U.S. District Court in Chattanooga alleging that TVA had violated the National Environmental Policy Act during the preparation of the Environmental Impact Statement. We asked Judge Frank Wilson to stop construction on Ocoee No. 2. At one point, our lawyer Charlie Warfield took us into the judge's chambers. On his wall was a photograph of Judge Wilson and his son running the whitewater rapids on the Nantahala River in a canoe.

The Battle Lines Are Drawn

A few weeks later Judge Wilson ruled that TVA had violated the National Environmental Policy Act by failing to consider the plan to charge fees to paddlers for water releases and required them to reconsider and rewrite the EIS. But he did not stop the project's construction. The lawsuit enhanced ORC's stature and sustained media attention throughout 1981. It did nothing to free the river from TVA's grip. TVA would revise the EIS in 1982 and move ahead with the project.

The lawsuit had one other benefit to the future of whitewater recreation. TVA argued that whitewater recreation was not a purpose of the Ocoee project, which planted a seed that eventually led to a revolutionary victory in other whitewater wars in the eastern U.S.

Around this time TVA's credibility was also eroding as press reports leaked out about the travails of Watts Bar and TVA's other nuclear projects. The problems at the Ocoee No. 2 project: the delays, labor strikes, and cost overruns fell into a similar pattern later found to afflict TVA's nuclear projects. Word of project delays and strikes began to trickle into the Gulf station. J.T. and his partners had acquired the station in 1981, paving over the grease spot and providing a conduit for information about the travails of Ocoee No. 2's reconstruction. Each construction blunder at Ocoee No. 2 got to the wire services and appeared in newspapers across the state. Gradually, the Ocoee No. 2 project looked less and less like the cheap hydropower TVA had been claiming.

JT Lemons, Rep. John Duncan, Sr, and David Brown, 1981

Yellow pine to rebuild the flume line had to be specially milled to 1913 specifications to create a watertight seal. Some of it was milled improperly and rejected, creating delays. Theft was rampant. While paddling one day, Mike Miller, one of our kayaking friends, found a chainsaw in the woods near one of the rapids. Marc returned it to the foreman at Jones Hailey, the construction company rebuilding the flume line, who said it was the 67th chainsaw stolen from the project.

The Battle Lines Are Drawn

As news about TVA's generating overcapacity and the problems of their nuclear program accumulated in the media, TVA's sacrosanct standing with the public began to erode. Despite TVA's lost luster, nothing short of a miracle would stop construction of Ocoee No. 2's wooden flume line. Our lawsuit suit was set aside in 1983 by the 6th Circuit Court of Appeals. Reconstruction of the flume line continued unabated.

We fought on, pushing every button we could, raising money and coalescing support by producing river festivals and promoting them to paddling clubs and the rafting community. The 1981 Ocoee River Festival was relatively small, attended by fewer than 1,000 paddlers. For me, the highlight was "Smoke's Kissing Booth". Smoke was a tall wiry guide at Ocoee Outdoors. He set up the booth without asking. Why stop him because after all, I thought, who would pay to kiss Smoke? An attractive female raft guide liked the idea and volunteered for a while, so it raised a few bucks, mostly from patrons who paid more if they did not have to kiss Smoke. I never asked Smoke for an honest accounting of the proceeds, but he turned in one hundred dollars. Later in the evening, Perception Kayaks honored me with their first-ever Conservationists of the Year Award.

The next year the 1982 Ocoee River Festival was the largest of all the Ocoee events with close to 4,000 in attendance. We used J.T.'s Ocoee Outdoors property. Unbeknownst to me J.T. convinced his relatives in the radio business in Chattanooga to promote the event.

THE WHITEWATER WARS

As the crowd swelled to over 4,000 strong, my only wish was that TVA could see it. At least, Curbow would know; he lived next door.

The festival took place on August 14th. It was hot. The crowd grew to fill the adjoining pasture. The sun was a huge red ball stewing above the tree line in the steamy vapors of late afternoon when a skydiver swooped in with an American flag flying from his left leg as he landed in an adjacent field. Later, the accomplished bluegrass musicians "Hiwassee Ridge" mesmerized the crowd with sweet harmonies of "Fox on the Run". As everyone was leaving, the whump of a fireworks mortar was heard followed by a single burst of a star shell over Curbow's house. I had met a guy a couple of months earlier who had the mortar and said he would shoot a star shell at the end of the Festival. I had forgotten all about it. It was a fitting end to a magical evening.

Wyatt Andrews from CBS News was there during the day for an interview. I had been up cooking barbeque chicken all night to sell at the festival. Andrews showed up for the interview at 11:00 AM. Most of what I said was unintelligible except for the short clips that appeared in his story on the Nightly News anchored by Bill Kurtis the following Sunday evening.

In the story, which ran for several minutes, TVA Director Richard Freeman portrayed us as a bunch of yahoos trying to take food out of the mouths of old women living on Social Security to pay for our recreational water releases. I countered that TVA had admitted in their EIS that the entire annual net benefits of the project were not noticeable in power rates, therefore some small measure for recreation would be less noticeable. TVA staged a shot of four men manually opening a gate in the dam for the water release as if they had to do it every day, when in fact the river flowed continuously without that action. The project's gates were remotely operated from Knoxville.

The River Trip

Despite our efforts, by the winter of 1983 the flume line was slated for completion that Fall. Hundreds of letters to Congress, rocking river festivals, and numerous trips by politicians vowing support for the river had produced nothing more than photo ops. Newspapers throughout the state editorialized in support of the continuation of Ocoee whitewater. Some urged TVA to kill the Ocoee project altogether. Nevertheless, after our lawsuit lost on appeal, no political solution had emerged. We began to think the river was going down the tubes, literally. It was a dark winter.

Then out of the blue, Jerry Mallet called from Denver. I had met Jerry, Executive Director of the Western River Guides Association, at their annual meeting in Salt Lake City. We had worked together on a Forest Service issue that Jerry led to a successful resolution in 1982. Jerry said he had a spot for me on a raft trip on the Colorado River through the Grand Canyon. Tennessee's Governor Lamar Alexander was scheduled to be on the trip. Jerry would hold me a spot for $600 dollars.

Several months earlier, J.T. Lemons and I were visiting Nashville for a tourism event. On a whim, he said let's drop by to see Tom Ingram, the governor's chief of staff whom J.T. had guided down the river with Governor

The River Trip

Alexander. Ingram stepped out to see us for a brief minute and delivered a key lesson, "you have to get directly to the Governor on this issue." All our meetings with politicians and agency folks had been getting platitudinous statements of support but little real action. Meanwhile I forged on, traveling the state, racking up resolution after resolution from Chambers of Commerce, Tourism Boards, and local governments, laying the groundwork for a political solution. The river trip with Governor Alexander was our last real hope for arriving at a viable solution.

With Ingram's advice ringing in my ears, I sent in my check to Jerry and met him in Denver that July. We drove to Flagstaff with my red Perception Dancer kayak loaned to me by Bill Masters on the camper top. On the day of the launch at Lee's Ferry, Governor Alexander was nowhere to be found. Jerry assured me he was hiking in for the last half of river and indeed we met on the Bright Angel Trail just short of Phantom Ranch. The Governor's eyes rolled when I introduced myself. He succeeded in arresting his jaw drop. But I could see the gears turning in his head, "who invited this guy on my vacation?"

From Phantom Ranch the river trip proceeded normally except that Jerry's plan for meals on the second half of the trip, the part most important to the future of the Ocoee, was nonexistent. At least no one was in charge. And Jerry forgot to bring the Governor a tent, which only amplified his wife's disdain for camping. With only a sleeping sack I was no help. One of the other kayakers, Randy Udall, and I rummaged through the lockers of the Canyoneers' raft every night to find enough cans of sloppy joe sauce and hamburger buns to keep everyone from starving. This was not a real outfitted trip, but a private trip and a funding raising effort for one of Jerry's conservation efforts. Canyoneers had loaned him a raft and crew but they were only working the first half of the trip. On the second half we still had the raft, but we were on our own logistically.

While we were setting up for camp one night deep in the Canyon, the racket of a helicopter descended upon us bearing his most regal highness, the Grand Canyon National Park Superintendent. At some point during the evening conversation the Superintendent divulged how much he enjoyed managing a real National Park like Grand Canyon instead of some eastern Park like the Great Smoky Mountains. The Superintendent should have done his homework. Governor Alexander grew up hiking the Great Smoky Mountains National Park which was a stone's throw from his hometown of Maryville, Tennessee.

The chopper arrived the next morning to take "the Super" back to his air-conditioned office. Peter Benchley, the author of Jaws had been on the trip to that point and flew out with him.

After this turn of events, I wondered if the Ocoee's chances for a political solution were going down the tubes in the Grand Canyon. I was crestfallen as night fell that evening. As the trip headed deeper into the Canyon, it seemed like it was rushing with irreversible energy into an abyss of impolitic events. I still had to figure out how to present the immediate loss of the Ocoee River to the Governor without trampling on the real purpose of his trip: the family's vacation.

The River Trip

Little did I know, the Governor was having the time of his life despite our amateurism or perhaps because of it. He enjoyed rescuing his boatman's oar after he botched the cheat of Crystal Rapid, which had been revised earlier that summer by a flash flood.

As we were stopped for lunch one day on a sandbar, I was conversing about the Ocoee with U.S. Representatives Tim Wirth and Jim Cooper who were on the trip. The conversation was in lieu of another peanut butter and jelly sandwich Randy had dug out of the raft's lockers. Overhearing my conversation with the two Democrats, Governor Alexander was compelled to engage. He walked over. "What's this about the Ocoee?" he said.

"Governor, the Ocoee is going down the tubes in a couple of months," I said. The flume was scheduled to begin operation within 2 months. After describing a few more details, Governor Alexander said he would call Senator Howard Baker, who had, after the 1982 election, ascended to Senate Majority leader. We had a plan. There was hope. Perhaps three years of my life and the tireless contributions of countless others had not been wasted.

I left Arizona and returned to West Virginia. I was splitting time between a new campaign to save the Gauley River in West Virginia and my apartment in Ocoee, Tennessee. I had developed a smoking habit that found me going through a pack of cigarettes on some days, interspersed by periods of abstinence and running. The anticipation and stress were taking its toll.

Negotiating for Peace and Water Releases

While we were waiting for the political deal to play out there was one last twist. Earlier in 1983, Marc and I attended a TVA board meeting in Cleveland, Tennessee where I made a conciliatory statement, appealing to the TVA board to provide water releases once the flume line was completed. Once again, I appealed for TVA to redesignate the Ocoee No. 2 project as a "multiple purpose" project to include recreation, which would eliminate the need for strict reimbursement for lost power when TVA provided recreational releases. The board hardly looked up from their perch on the stage. After the meeting, to console me perhaps, one of TVA's Ocoee No. 2 employees, stopped us in the parking lot.

"That was the smartest thing I have ever heard you say," he told me. "They called me up one day and said we'll shoot David Brown for one thousand dollars, but I told them 'no'. We don't want to go that far."

Was I supposed to be grateful? Or maybe he was just insulting me by putting such a low price on my life. That was my first reaction. In retrospect, I think he was trying to offer an olive branch because he thought they had won the battle. Our goal had never been to stop reconstruction of the flume line. It was just to get water releases. The antipathy of a handful of local TVA employees toward the ORC's efforts was understandable given their perceived threat to their jobs. They just went too far at times.

Another crazy event occurred in those last months of the battle that underscored Polk County's status as place on the edge of modern times. I was in the little Ocoee post office when a massive explosion rocked the building. An illegal M-80 fireworks factory blew up just down the road from Sunburst, Marc Hunt's outfitting businesses. Eleven people died in the explosion. Their body parts hung about in the trees. One worker was blown into the sky and crashed through the roof of a nearby house. It made me wonder if there was a connection to the fellow who shot the fireworks at our Ocoee River Festival the year before.

In the summer of 1983, Steve Taylor, a scientist and consultant for NASA whom I had met while working on the Gauley River project, did a cost benefit analysis of the Ocoee No. 2 rehabilitation project which revealed that it was not cost effective. The resulting article made big news in the Nashville Tennessean and was undoubtedly read by everyone of consequence in Governor Alexander's Administration. Tish Jenkins' response for TVA did not really refute the analysis; she said something to affect that hindsight was 20/20 and recreation releases would only worsen the project's cost benefit ratio. I was quoted as saying she sounded like Alice in Wonderland, which she probably never forgot.

Congressman Jim Cooper would later tell us that the article informed politicians that we knew what we were doing. The article and TVA's response further undermined their position. Two years later, Steve Taylor would be hired as an expert witness by the flume line contractor Jones-Hailey in its lawsuit against TVA.

On Labor Day weekend 1983, exactly seven years after the flume was shut down and recreational whitewater flows had begun, TVA once again opened the gate to the flume line and started diverting the Ocoee's water from the riverbed. The riverbed was dry and the river's outfitting industry was in crisis. With a very uncertain future, outfitters and kayakers were praying for a solution.

After the Grand Canyon trip, Governor Alexander did call Senator Baker as he said he would. We knew they were working on a solution but had little to no contact with anyone until the Commissioner of Conservation for Tennessee, Charles Howell, called in October and asked me to meet him at the TVA Office of Power on a Saturday to negotiate the Ocoee deal. Marc and David Broemel joined us. We arrived on a gray day and rode the elevator up a few floors to a conference room. Apparently, Senator Baker's office had already come up with a game plan so TVA knew how much money they would get for water releases for the next 35 years. Our job was to get as many days of water as possible.

TVA's phalanx of lawyers, public relations warriors, and number crunchers were spread out around a large u-shaped table. I counted eleven at one point.

Negotiating for Peace and Water Releases

Commissioner Howell, Marc, Broemel and I sat together on one side. In the early days of the Ocoee battle, I had read a newspaper article in which Philip Habib, the Reagan Administration's negotiator for the Middle East, stated that any successful negotiation required negotiating from a position of power. The State of Tennessee represented our powerful ally. We had no chance negotiating directly with TVA without the State's backing. I had been cultivating the state to play that role for three years. Still, eleven to four did not feel like great odds even with Senator Baker and the Governor behind us.

It was a little hard to figure out what was going on between Parris and Howell, who were doing most of the talking. TVA was intent on limiting releases to something like 84 days, which they had evaluated in their Environmental Impact Statement. Commissioner Howell was not happy.

At one point, Parris and Howell were parrying back and forth over the number of days when Howell blasted Parris, "I thought you were a big enough man to come here to make a deal," he roared. Parris' face immediately went crimson. Parris called for an adjournment and TVA's contingent ran off to their little ante room to regroup and figure out how to respond. I wondered if the negotiation was over.

It was not. After more discussion, we broke again. Howell gave us a calendar. Marc and I marked off the specific days and hours for the releases, which would number 116 instead of 84. Someone in tourism had told the state 110 days were the minimum necessary for a return on investment. Marc made sure private boaters got days that would be important for them during the dry months when other rivers with natural flows were unavailable.

As if to make up for irritating Howell, TVA offered six additional maintenance days. At the time TVA used the temporary shutdown to flush sludge out of the intakes at Ocoee No. 3, a project just upstream of Ocoee No. 2. Sediment from the run-off from the denuded Copper Basin had all but filled the lake behind the No. 3 dam, requiring TVA to clear the diversion intakes periodically. Never mind, those six days in September were unusable for commercial rafting since the river was the consistency of melted chocolate while sludge was being washed down the river.

Later, TVA would be forced to cease the sludge release by water quality laws making those days viable for paddling. Fish would return to the river until the agency had an "accident" in 2009, releasing more sludge from No. 3 which resulted in a massive fish kill. TVA had to run high flows for several days to wash the mud out of the river into Parksville Lake downstream.

With the agreement signed in 1984, we lost about two hundred cubic feet per second from the flows we had grown accustomed to when the flume line was not operating. Marc and TVA's Jay Jensen got into an argument during the negotiation over the flow. Jensen claimed 1,200 cubic feet per second (cfs) was normal.

Marc insisted it was 1,400, which probably included natural flow from tributary creeks. TVA bullied us into accepting 1,200 by claiming we would enjoy the same flows since the flume's decommissioning. That was not true.

One aspect of the arrangement we had not anticipated was that Governor Alexander and Commissioner Howell were adamant that the Ocoee would be managed as a State Park unit, which was included in the finalized agreement. The document provided easements to the State for the property necessary to operate and manage the State Park. The Governor and Howell were not ready to trust TVA with the recreational future of the Ocoee any more than we were. Their foresight and the state investments in river access facilities, restrooms, outfitter permits, and ranger operations resulted in a truly outstanding recreation opportunity for years to come.

After our negotiation in December of 1983 at the behest of Senator Howard Baker, Congress passed an appropriations bill with $7.4 million included in it to pay for water releases on the Ocoee for 35 years. The stars had aligned ever so briefly for a legislative solution.

There had been a battle over the appropriation, which the New York Times would later label as "pork" in their dig at Senator Baker. Someone was still working against the deal on the House of Representatives side, but fortunately Senator Baker prevailed in conference committee when the House and Senate reconciled the differences in their two versions of the continuing appropriations bill.

THE WHITEWATER WARS

In March of 1984 TVA signed a 35-year contract with the State of Tennessee to provide water releases for 116 days per year for the next 35 years. The Ocoee No. 2 project, originally authorized in 1978 by the TVA board at a cost of $14.7 million, ended up costing the agency over $40 million. A General Accounting Office study published in 1984 revealed that TVA had not adequately accounted for all the project costs, including a lawsuit by the project's contractor which was quietly settled two years after the project was completed. Nonetheless, the deal was done, and it worked. By 2018 outfitters had reimbursed the Treasury for the entire amount of the appropriation with fees collected annually by TVA.

I closed my apartment and left the Ocoee for good in the Fall of 1983 to devote full-time to the campaign to save the Gauley River. I returned to the Ocoee in 1984 to paddle and visit friends. In July of that year, I found the river to be a mere shadow of its former glory. TVA was releasing 1,000 cubic feet per second (cfs) or less instead of the 1,200 cfs in the agreement. The agreement provided for an average flow of 1,200 cfs over a 60-day period but it could never be less than 1,000 cfs. TVA was averaging in high water flows from uncontrollable rain events during the 60 days, which gave them wiggle room to reduce flows during dryer periods. I wrote Commissioner Howell a letter expressing my disappointment. He must have gotten to work on it, because shortly thereafter TVA stopped shaving water and began releasing the agreed to flow rate. Without the State of Tennessee's involvement in the agreement, paddlers and outfitters would have been behind the 8 ball.

During the negotiation, I insisted that the payback be based on 60,000 raft customers. By the end of the century more than 200,000 rafters visited the river each year, so the fee needed to payback the Treasury was reduced to $1.00 per person for a time. The contract provided for an adjustment, which was helpful on a river where price competition kept the price of the trip low.

In later years outfitters and paddlers would win again on flows through the Olympic course on the upper section of the river above the Ocoee No. 2 dam. The State, TVA and the U.S. Forest Service had invested $28 million to build a state-of-the-art whitewater slalom course and conduct the whitewater slalom racing competition as part of the 1996 Olympics in nearby Atlanta. But remarkably despite that investment there were no plans for water releases for the continuation of whitewater paddling after the event. After the 1996 Olympic event, the Forest Service asked me to set up testing of various flows in anticipation of ongoing recreational releases. We tested three different levels and paddlers agreed 1,600 cfs was the best experience, which became the standard flow for the upper Ocoee through the Olympic course. But it took years for outfitters to arrive at a reliable water release schedule and the fees required to reimburse TVA for lost power were so high the trip on that section of river was marginally profitable when compared to their operations on the popular middle Ocoee.

Exceeding Expectations

Fast forward to 2017. 40 years after the river's rebirth, the 7 millionth paddler took a trip down the Ocoee River. The river had generated millions in economic benefits to Polk and nearby Bradley Counties. Most in Polk County recognize tourism as their growth industry after reaching an accommodation with "the rafters". The Copper Basin is a green oasis reforested by the TVA and the company hired to clean-up the old, denuded superfund site. The surrounding mountain tops are designated wilderness. The 1996 Atlanta Olympic kayak competition, which no one would have predicted in 1980, had come and gone. The Olympic site on the Upper Ocoee is surrounded by mountain bike trails and campgrounds. Today, the Ocoee River is the center piece of a recreation and economic renaissance that will only become more important as the economic boom in the southeast and I-75 corridor devour more flatland and greenspace.

Visitors will come and go, but the value of the Ocoee and surrounding National Forest will be worshipped for decades to come. Or so we thought.

To the dismay of many, storm clouds gathered over the Ocoee River once more as the 35-year contract between TVA and the state of Tennessee, which was signed in 1984, was set to expire in 2018. To renew the water release contract, TVA's official position was that outfitters would have to pay $9 million up front for the first five years of releases. Where were outfitters going to get $9 million? Incredulously, TVA stuck to that position for over 2 years, telling outfitters it was nonnegotiable. A new Environmental Impact Statement would be needed. Complicating matters, the Forest Service also wanted to issue permits to outfitters. While Polk County had changed, TVA's culture was still grinding away in its opposition to whitewater recreation on the Ocoee.

In response to the new challenge, the Ocoee River Council was revived in the winter of 2015. I volunteered for two years to direct the effort funded by America Outdoors, the national association of outfitters I had led for 27 years. Stacy Stone, an expert paddler and natural organizer, was hired to execute a grassroots campaign to gain support for the river. By the summer of 2016 Stacy had collected and sent over 5,000 letters to Congress in support of whitewater recreation, which eventually made their way to Governor. She secured over a dozen resolutions from Chambers of Commerce and local governments in the counties surrounding the river which were sent to Congress and the Governor.

We went to the media early to let the public know the river was at risk. In three months, the new ORC generated more publicity and grassroots support than in the first two years of the original ORC in the early 1980's. We were not amateurs anymore. Internet blogs, email, and websites provided information at the speed of light, advancing the pace of the controversy, and giving a nimble organization a fighting chance. The successful experience of the original Ocoee battle from 1980 to 1983 provided a template for the new campaign.

For those of us who have watched the Ocoee River turn into a rural economic development success and inspire millions with its whitewater experience, the uncertainty over the river's future was a little hard to swallow.

The agency's culture had still not accepted whitewater recreation as a legitimate purpose of the Ocoee No. 2 project. At the time, their embrace of rural economic development did not include small businesses and whitewater recreation. Congress was still reluctant to provide much oversight of TVA. During the outset of this second Ocoee battle, the legislative director for one Senator said, in a stunning admission of Congressional contrition, that even if they passed legislation to provide water for whitewater recreation, TVA would ignore the legislation.

TVA had already proven that its position requiring strict reimbursement for lost power was discretionary, only applicable, apparently, to whitewater recreation. The evidence was publicized in the Spring of 2015 when TVA and Senator Lamar Alexander, took credit for a deal which cost TVA millions from power revenues to support non-native trout fisheries in the tailwaters of 13 projects. Annual power losses and other expenses to provide flows suitable to trout fishermen cost the agency $3 to $4 million annually for about the same economic benefit that Ocoee whitewater produced at one location. In May 2015 TVA also announced a deal to fund three fish hatcheries from power revenues to the tune of $1 million annually. A little payback, perhaps to the trout fishermen displaced by the Tellico Dam.

The groundswell of support for the Ocoee would eventually result in TVA reducing its demand for revenue to $11 million for a 15-year period. Brian Bivens, the outfitters' lobbyist, developed legislation with the State to save the river once again and provide for continued management of the Ocoee River as a State Park. Outfitters will pay the state ten percent of gross revenues per year over the 15-year period to offset the State's $11 million payment to TVA to provide water releases. The Ocoee was saved again and this time the agreement included releases through Olympic course on the upper Ocoee, a monumental win. One of the greatest achievements was that TVA entered into a partnership with paddlers, the State, and the Forest Service to make the agreement and whitewater recreation on the Ocoee a long-term success.

THE WHITEWATER WARS

As a recreation resource the Ocoee River was too important to be put to death inside the historic flume line. As the population of the Southeast grows and Nashville evolves into the next congested big city, the Ocoee River, the nearby Hiwassee, and the surrounding mountains of the Cherokee National Forests will continue to provide an escape from the daily grind for years to come.

The Gauley River Battle
1983 to 1987

Pillow Rock, Gauley River, Whitewater Photography, Fayetteville, WV

Arriving in West Virginia

Sunlight dappled the parking lot of Wildwater Unlimited as I pulled into Thurmond, West Virginia on a brilliant summer day. It was July 1983. My possessions were tucked away in the smallest covered trailer available for rent from U-Haul. I would not realize how special the day was until a few months later. Jon Dragan, the owner of Wildwater, had offered to help me move into an apartment in Oak Hill.

The Ocoee battle, although still looking forward to its most important political development, was winding down. The trip with Tennessee's Governor Alexander on the Colorado River through the Grand Canyon was three weeks away. West Virginia outfitters had decided to provide funding to employ me and take over the effort to save the Gauley River from a proposed Corps of Engineers' hydro project. Since I was already running the Eastern Professional River Outfitters Association (EPRO), the job was a natural fit.

I was comfortable and confident on that July day despite my humble financial status. Frank Lukacs, a West Virginia outfitter, had hired me to run EPRO, a small trade association of about 80 outfitters. Together the income from two jobs provided enough salary to live modestly. The Gauley River deserved no less than a full commitment regardless of the compensation, a sentiment I never regretted. I was honored to be leading the effort to save it.

The Gauley River is the most beautiful river in the eastern United States. The Corps' proposed long tunnel diversion project would divert water from the existing Summersville Dam through a tunnel in the sandstone around the upper three miles of the river to generators in a powerhouse at Pillow Rock rapid. The project would raise the lake elevation by 16 feet to provide sufficient hydrostatic head and water capacity to make the project cost effective.

Jon Dragan had started Wildwater Expeditions Unlimited with his brothers Tom and Chris in 1968. He was a pioneer and the king of the West Virginia whitewater rafting industry. Every outfitter on the New River paid to take out their rafts on his property at Fayette Station at the end of the 12-mile trip down the New River. Vast land holding companies and remnants of the mining companies that once dominated the New River Gorge repelled efforts by interlopers to buy access to the river. Wildwater owned the only New River takeout in 1983. That would change a couple of years later when a group of outfitters developed a take-out at Teays just downstream of Fayette Station. At the time, Dragan was probably making as much money on his takeout as on his rafting business.

As the story goes, Dragan had cut a deal with Lance Martin, the first whitewater rafting outfitter in the eastern U.S. He would stay in West Virginia if Lance would not compete with him from his operation on the Youghiogheny River in Pennsylvania. That agreement did not extend to Lance's guides. Some would start their own rafting companies among them Imre Szilagyi and John Connelly.

Lance Martin, Jim Greiner, and Jon Dragan on Chattooga River circa 1970. Wildwater Ltd. Photo

Dragan was not in the office when I arrived, so I wandered into the store. A rafting video loop was playing with Dragan and his crew paddling Avons, a brand of raft he did not own. I asked the store clerk, an attractive woman named Robin, what Jon was doing in an Avon, since he was a lifelong advocate of Demaree Inflatables. She said the video was from Costa Rica. Robin and I would marry 15 months later in an outdoor wedding at Carnifex Ferry State Park overlooking the Gauley's Pillow Rock rapid.

David Broemel, one of the pillars of the Ocoee defense team, had taken me to West Virginia in the early spring of 1981 to run the Gauley River. As we crossed the gorge on the New River Bridge, at the time the world's longest single arch span, my jaw dropped at the beauty of the 900-foot-deep crack in the Appalachian Plateau. West Virginia's rivers were incomparable and a great tourist attraction in a rural and impoverished state dependent on coal mining. In the early 1980's with interest in whitewater rafting on the upsurge, customers would drive many hours for a day trip down the New or Gauley River. It was still early in the product cycle for whitewater rafting. In those days, rain, high water, and chilly weather could not deter demand for West Virginia's rafting experience.

The U.S Army Corps of Engineers controlled most of the water projects in the mid-Atlantic region. They were built in the era after World War II, when the Army's engineering bureaucracy sought to maintain its status and employment by building dams. The Corps had been involved in civil works since the 19th Century. As the years progressed, they sought new missions to include dams and flood control projects which would have to be authorized and later funded by Congress.

The origins of the Corps of Engineers can be traced to the Revolutionary War and the Continental Congress when engineers were needed to build fortifications and bridges. George Washington appointed the first engineers in the Army on June 16, 1775. It was not until 1802 that Congress officially authorized the Corps as a branch of the Army. Today, the Department of Civil Works with its own Assistant Secretary controls its non-military projects, which include navigation, flood control, water supply, and activities to support aquatic ecosystems. Congress loves the Corps of Engineers because it is a conduit through which important federal projects are delivered to their Congressional districts. According to the Congressional Research Service "Congress typically funds USACE (U.S. Army Corps of Engineers) above the President's request. For fiscal year 2020, Congress provided $7.65 billion (54% above the FY2020 request). The love affair with the West Virginia Congressional delegation would be interrupted by the Gauley River battle in the 1980's.

Most of the commercially viable whitewater rivers in the East benefit from water stored in large reservoirs behind Corps of Engineers or utility company dams, an unintended consequence of their construction. The Youghiogheny, the Lehigh, the New, and the Gauley were the most prominent whitewater rivers in the mid-Atlantic region dependent on water releases from Corps' projects.

The Summersville Dam on the Gauley River controls flows into its magnificent canyon. The Summersville Lake Project was built under the Army Corps of Engineers' supervision between 1960 and 1966 at a cost of nearly 48 million dollars. The project was authorized by Congress for flood control and low flow augmentation. President Lyndon Johnson and his wife Lady Bird dedicated the project in September 1966.

Arriving in West Virginia

Like the Tennessee Valley Authority, by the late 1970's the Corps was running out of sites for new dams. There was newfound hope for their engineers in reworking existing projects to add capacity for water supply, flood control and hydroelectric power generation. At the same time engineering consultants had won the opportunity to retrofit the same projects with private or municipally owned hydro projects, which had to be licensed through the Federal Energy Regulatory Commission (FERC). It was a matter of who got their project approved and funded first, the Corps or private hydro consultants. Both initiatives would present a challenge to whitewater recreation on the Gauley River.

Jennings Randolph with Lyndon B. Johnson, Ladybird Johnson, and Hulett Smith at Summersville Dam Dedication, September 3, 1966, Senator Jennings Randolph Collection, West Virginia State Archives.

The looks on their faces are as if on that day someone asked them, "do you think this dam will ever be authorized to enhance downstream whitewater recreation?"

The Brain Trust

I had agreed to move to the Gauley to head up the effort to save it while I was wrapping up the Ocoee solution. The volunteer effort led by local paddlers, which had created Citizens for Gauley River (CFGR) in 1982, had been effective but not complete or as robust as having professional staff to coordinate the effort. The Corps still had their foot on the throttle, seeking authorization and funding for the modification to Summersville Dam. Volunteers were simply not able to coordinate outfitters, private boaters, and politicians in their spare time.

The first task was assembling a brain trust to provide the expertise necessary to win the political, legal, and public relations battle. Before I moved to West Virginia, Dragan suggested I talk to Charlie Walbridge, a well-known paddler from Pennsylvania with ties to private boaters and outfitters. Charlie began his professional career in whitewater while working for the Nantahala Outdoor Center in Bryson City, North Carolina in 1974. Like many northerners, Charlie's skepticism about the South evaporated shortly after his arrival. Many northerners had developed bad impressions of the region during the civil rights battles of the 1960s. Then, the movie Deliverance, added to their perturbation that the rural south was crude

The Brain Trust

and primitive. Deliverance was a fictional depiction of the backwoods, but unless you had visited the South, you really would not know that.

I faced this kind of skepticism about southerners throughout my career -- never with Charlie though. His wise counsel and support helped give creditability to my efforts. I called him in the winter of 1983 to assemble a brain trust for the Gauley River effort.

The Gauley River's beauty and power attracted enormous talent to its defense. Among the names Charlie gave me was Pope Barrow, a lawyer in the legislative counsel's office in the U.S. House of Representatives. Pope drafted the bills that members of Congress introduced and voted into law. Steve Taylor, a number crunching scientist, did much of the hydrology work on the Gauley. There were others, paddling clubs and outfitters who helped fund the efforts with relentless contributions. David Arnold and Jeff Proctor had close ties to the politicians in the state. It was their relationship with Congressman Nick Joe Rahall (D-WV) that provided key political support. Then there was Congressman Rahall's irascible legislative director Jim Zoia. Without him our legislative efforts would have been dead in the water.

Frank Lukacs, who hired me to run the Eastern Professional River Outfitters Association, Paul Breuer, who gave us use of his campground for the Gauley River Festival, and many others added power and financial support to our effort.

THE WHITEWATER WARS

My first experience with river conservation had been as a volunteer in a futile effort to stop a dam on the Savannah River where I overcame post-Vietnam war funk by canoe camping along the last undammed stretch of the Savannah in the rocky Piedmont Region of northeast Georgia. That experience and the legal challenges we pursued during the Ocoee project gave me a fundamental idea that we could retroactively make downstream recreation a project purpose for the Summersville Dam on the Gauley River. During our lawsuit to save the Ocoee, TVA had argued that recreation was not an official project purpose for the Ocoee No. 2 project, therefore providing water releases for recreation would pull the thread that unraveled the entire financial underpinnings of the agency.

It was the winter of 1983 when I cold called Pope Barrow about joining the CFGR board. I sensed a bit of skepticism. During the call I told him about the idea to make downstream recreation a project purpose to give the Corps of Engineers the authority to provide water releases. My suggestion was met with a pause; so, I moved on. A few weeks later a draft bill to make whitewater recreation a purpose of the Summersville Dam was circulated by Congressman Rahall. We had tried to get this done on the Ocoee, but it never got traction, and we did not have the political power to override TVA's objections.

The Corps thought they had inviolate political leverage over the outfitters by withholding water releases for the Gauley season until the last minute. The Fall water releases on the Gauley were incidental to and dependent upon the fall drawdown of Summersville Dam to provide winter flood control capacity. The drawdown created an epic whitewater season when few other rivers were running. But the releases were dependent upon the availability of water from Summersville and in dry years the Corps would augment flows in the Kanawha River basin to maintain water quality there. Low flow augmentation during a dry summer meant there was less water behind the dam for the Fall Gauley season. To gain support for their proposed project, the Corps promised reliable flows upon completion of the long tunnel project.

The Corps would show up at a meeting in August each year to let the outfitters know how much water was available for Fall Gauley season which began the first weekend after Labor Day. Outfitters had already booked conditional reservations, which had to be confirmed after the Corps' gave them the green light for the season. Don Herndon from the Corps' Huntington office ran the show.

Outfitters were split initially on the approach to a solution to this water release conundrum, so I was walking a tightrope. Outfitters had a good working relationship with the Corps. I was a threat to it. There was never a doubt on the track. Despite the Corps' promises to provide more water if their project was completed, the sacrifices necessary would never be worth it. The Gauley's river canyon, unrivaled in beauty by any other in the United States, deserved protection.

THE WHITEWATER WARS

Adventures on the Gorge

I set up the CFGR office amongst the boxes containing my few possessions in an apartment in Oak Hill, West Virginia. A few items had been left behind at each stop along the way as I had moved around the country over the previous four years. Moving to Oak Hill consisted of unloading a chest of drawers, a mattress, filing cabinet with a bullet hole through the top drawer, a desk and a couple of chairs. How the bullet hole got there is a mystery. I acquired the filing cabinet while living in Polk County, Tennessee. It looked like someone had put a loaded gun in the top drawer and it went off when they slammed the drawer shut.

Aside from organizing the CFGR board, the other important task would be establishing the Gauley River Festival. The Festival would bring the diverse supporters

The Brain Trust

together from around the nation to celebrate the river and have fun while contributing to saving it. The festival on the Ocoee had been a great success. The formula was simple: music plus paddlers and beer equals a successful event. In September 1983, the first Gauley River Festival was held in a driving rain at Burnwood Campground next to the New River Gorge. Congressman Bob Wise showed up to address a few hundred hearty paddlers assembled there. Jim Zoia came over from Washington. We raised a few hundred dollars for CFGR.

Our efforts to save the river began getting publicity in the Charleston papers. Skip Johnson, the outdoors writer for the Charleston Gazette, was fair but clearly a hook and bullet guy who was generally supportive of projects that promoted hunting and fishing. Governor Rockefeller's Administration supported the proposed Corps' project because the Corps had promised to provide low flows in the upper three miles of the river for a put-and-take trout fishery, which the State's Department of Natural Resources wanted. DNR's fishery guys also opposed water releases on the Gauley because, as one of them told me, rainbow trout did not evolve in those conditions. Ironically, rainbow trout did not evolve in any eastern river. The only trout native to eastern streams was brook trout.

Crunching the Numbers and the Corps

We had our work cut out for us to overcome a powerful wall of political support for the project. In-state grassroots political support would be necessary to give Congressman Rahall the political cover necessary to pursue a legislative solution. That was my job along with coordinating our political capital. The outfitters, especially Dave Arnold, Jeff Proctor, and Jon Dragan had already developed tremendous goodwill for the outfitting industry and many connections throughout the state that would provide support for our cause. In my career, no other outfitter group had better political standing than West Virginia outfitters, except possibly Idaho outfitters in the early days.

One of our first plays was to alert the United Mine Workers to the hydro project, which would detract from the use of coal. It was a minor challenge to them, but any level of political support from a powerful political constituency was important at this stage. The original CFGR volunteers pulled that off as we began our campaign. We later convinced Trout Unlimited to support our position undermining West Virginia DNR.

Crunching the Numbers and the Corps

In 1983 the Corps was playing hard ball by withholding water and abbreviating the Fall drawdown. Don Herndon met with the outfitters in August 1983 at the Bridgetender Inn near the New River Gorge bridge. He explained that water storage was low due to the Corps' need to augment flows in the Kanawha for water quality. The Gauley season would be shortened significantly.

The outfitters were fried since they already had reservations which would have to be cancelled or moved. Steve Taylor's hydrological analysis later revealed that the Corps had mismanaged water that year. Some of us thought it was on purpose.

Outfitters organized a letter writing campaign to their customers and to members of Congress. Class VI published the Colonel's Huntington District phone number in a mailing to their customers prompting dozens of calls from titans of industry, entertainers, and members of Congress. One call to the Colonel was from the CEO of Proctor and Gamble. A Corps' employee confided that it was more than the Colonel could handle.

The Corps took notice. It was late October when Don Herndon summoned me to a meeting near Charleston to discuss the proposed project. I thought the meeting would be a small, get acquainted meeting. Instead several of his staff and Skip Johnson from the Gazette were seated around the table in a conference room. I smelled set-up. Skip had obviously been briefed by Herndon prior to my arrival.

Herndon did not waste any time in getting to the purpose for the meeting. He opened by asking me if I was aware that the Corps had held a meeting with all the outfitters in Beckley where they agreed to support the Corps' long tunnel project. Herndon said CFGR's efforts were out of sync with the interest of the outfitting industry. This little set-up was done to undermine the support we were gaining in the press and my role.

What could I say? I told him I was unaware of any such meeting and did not believe his assertion that outfitters supported the project. The meeting was over in 15 minutes. I left wondering what kind of article would show up in the paper. Remarkably, Skip never wrote a word about it. Later I would learn from queries to several outfitters that no such meeting had taken place. One of the disappointing lessons from these battles is that you cannot trust federal agencies to be honest when they really want something. They would understate the costs, overstate the benefits, and misrepresent events to get what they wanted.

Early on, a win to secure Fall water releases was desperately needed to avoid erosion of support from the outfitters who were dependent upon the Corps' cooperation. I did not know how to get that done at the time, but it would be the number one goal in the back of my mind as the issue evolved. I needed to let the stew simmer for a while and get my feet on the ground.

We had some great political assets to bring to bear once we had a feasible solution to present. West Virginia's

Crunching the Numbers and the Corps

Senator Jennings Randolph was Chairman of the Senate Committee on Environment and Public Works. All roads to the Corps of Engineers in Congress went through his office.

Steve Taylor had been at work on the hydrology issues. He developed a scenario for operation of the Summersville Dam that would dramatically increase the reliability of the Fall drawdown by mimicking historical project operations. He had the solution in a few charts; flows could be pulsed from the project during dry years to provide releases for 21 days.

Standard Corps' practice was to draw water down from summer pool to the lower winter pool level by turning on the valve and letting the water run night and day until Summersville Lake reached winter pool. Taylor's solution was to turn the water off at night thereby extending the project's capacity to provide Fall recreation releases.

The Corps had responded to the proposal by singing their old song: because whitewater recreation was not a project purpose, modifying flows to benefit downstream recreation was not within their discretion and they could be sued for any bodily injury that resulted from their decision to provide recreational releases. We thought this was a bogus argument because federal agencies are granted immunity from claims for discretionary decisions that do not violate laws or regulations. By arguing they could not manage Gauley flows, the Corps was effectively limiting its own discretion.

THE WHITEWATER WARS

Rafters at Pillow Rock rapid, Whitewater Photography, Fayetteville, WV

In early 1984 I thought we should take a long shot and get a meeting with William Gianelli, the U.S. Army Corps of Engineers' Assistant Secretary for Civil Works in the Pentagon. He controlled Corps' programs and water projects. Some of Vice President George Bush's staff had been whitewater rafting on the New River with Wildwater. We could set up the meeting in the Pentagon through Senator Randolph (this was Dragan's idea) and then try to get help with Gianelli from the Vice President's staff. The threat of the legislation introduced by Congressman Rahall to modify the project's purpose to include downstream whitewater recreation would provide incentive to the Corps to formally implement a water release program. At least that was our hope.

Crunching the Numbers and the Corps

I raised the idea with Dragan, who immediately called Senator Randolph's office to get the meeting with Gianelli. It would take a month, but Dragan would not be denied. He knew how to pull the levers even though he was unable to attend the meeting.

We were going to take Steve's documentation and appeal to Assistant Secretary Gianelli to implement the water release regime by the using the fall drawdown to extend the economic benefits of the project with little increased costs.

It was Spring 1984. Steve Taylor, Frank Lukacs, and a couple of other outfitters joined me in the meeting with Gianelli. Going to a meeting in the Pentagon is not something everyone gets to do. We were in awe walking down the corridors of this massive structure, which was built in 16 months at the start of World War II.

Gianelli's receptionist ushered us into the conference room and the Assistant Secretary entered a few minutes later. He sat down with a note pad and glanced with his head half-cocked and said, "I know about you white river rafters. I was chairman of the water board on the Stanislaus River when that guy chained himself to the tree to keep us from filling the reservoir. What have you got for me?"

Getting a favorable outcome from this meeting was a long shot and this remark confirmed it. I had not done my homework.

Nonetheless, I feigned ignorance, although Mark Dubois, the conservationist who had chained himself to the tree, had been at an American Rivers meeting I attended. I optimistically offered our proposal to extend the project's economic benefits using available water resources. He may not have expected the economic angle from "white river rafters", given his experience in California. We intentionally avoided discussing the Corps' proposed project so as not to muddy the water. I turned it over to Steve to explain the concept of managing the water for the Fall Gauley season. His presentation was impeccably documented.

Gianelli was polite and said he would look at our proposal. The meeting broke up and we headed home without much hope for a favorable result given the politics. As the days ticked by, I all but forgot about the meeting. There really was not much we could do but hope.

Congressman Rahall gave momentum and justification for the Corps to plan for water releases in an obscure provision in the fiscal year 1985 Appropriations bill which passed Congress in July 1984. SEC. 107 stated, "Funds appropriated under any provision of law for the operation of the Summersville Lake, West Virginia Project shall be used to carry out all authorized project purposes of such project, including but not limited to whitewater recreation of the Gauley River downstream of such project." This was a backhanded authorization for whitewater recreation, which would later be passed in authorization legislation in 1986. As it was in an appropriations bill, the Corps might argue that it was only good for FY 1985. Our hope was that it was enough to convince the Corps to plan for whitewater releases. We would not know for sure until months later.

A New Hydro Threat Emerges

In the meantime, another threat arose as the Noah Corporation, a hydropower consulting firm, began to seriously consider putting a private hydroelectric project at the base of the Summersville Dam. While this project would not impact the gorge, it too could disrupt flows. Jim Price, the President of Noah, had convinced the city of Summersville, West Virginia, to participate as a beneficiary of the project.

In the introduction to a short booklet titled <u>SUMMERSVILLE HYDROELECTRIC POWER PLANT</u>, Noah President Jim Price described the prospects for their project this way.

"We set up Noah Corp. in 1980 to benefit from the law that passed in 1978, which required utilities to buy power from small power producers, which included hydroelectric projects less than 80 MW. After searching for existing dams that could be developed, we began to focus on existing federal dams in the eastern U.S., particularly in the Appalachian Mountains, where there were a number of flood control dams which did not have power generation facilities in place. We looked at federal projects in Virginia, West Virginia, Pennsylvania, Kentucky, Ohio, Indiana, etc. In considering the power

generating features of these dams, Summersville Dam stood heads above the crowd. It was being examined by the Army Corps of Engineers for a federal project and was receiving some consideration by private companies for development of hydropower. I first visited the site in July 1980. I was captured by the power potential as evidenced by the water rushing out of its penstocks (tubes) below the dam. It was so impressive. We did not know at that time how difficult, expensive, and time-consuming the development would be – with so many setbacks. We also had no idea of the multiple uses of the lake and Gauley River. At that time whitewater rafting was unknown as a commercial venture with anything like the public participation that now exists. The dream of developing power at that site, the potential profit and our feeling of accomplishment sustained us through the next 21 years until the hydroelectric plant was operating commercially. The potential of the Summersville Hydroelectric Project has captured the imagination and enthusiasm of several other key parties and individuals. It has so much potential compared to other available projects that it eventually gained the support of the various parties necessary to make it a reality."

Price signed an agreement with the City of Summersville for the proposed project in 1980. The Federal Energy Regulatory Commission (FERC) issued a preliminary permit in 1981, but it was withdrawn because the river was under study for potential federal Wild and Scenic River designation. Later, the City of Summersville would be granted a license from FERC after a challenge

A New Hydro Threat Emerges

from Manassas, Virginia failed. In 1995 in a complex arrangement with the City of Summersville, Catamount Energy Corp., a subsidiary of Central Vermont Public Service Company, agreed to finance and operate the project, receiving all revenue for the first 25 years. After delays, construction of the powerhouse at the foot of Summersville Dam began in 1999.

In 1984, we had to deal with this private project as well as the threat from the Corps' proposed project. The solution would be Rahall's legislation to retroactively designate downstream whitewater recreation as a project purpose and prescribe water releases during the Fall drawdown of the reservoir. Noah's hydro project, which would be licensed by the Federal Energy Regulatory Commission (FERC), would have to operate with whatever water the Corps provided. They would still be able to generate during the whitewater releases but the project's owners would not have any control over timing or flow volume. Hydro would not be a project purpose. Lake users did not want the project jacking the lake level around in the summer for hydro even if the City of Summersville was a beneficiary of the project.

To muddy the water, a battle emerged among outfitters that made me wonder if our efforts would blow-up altogether. Four outfitters - Class VI, North American, Mountain River Tours and Appalachian Wildwater - put together an extraordinary partnership and a plan to build a take-out below the New River Gorge Bridge on the New River at Teays' Landing. They would no longer have to pay tens of thousands of dollars annually to Jon

Dragan to use his takeout at Fayette Station. This was no minor project. It cost three quarters of a million dollars and required shutting down one of the nation's busiest rail lines for up to 72 hours. The project required ripping up the tracks and inserting a giant pipe tunnel in a trench, then covering it up for the tracks to be reset. The tracks were owned by the railroad company, CSX Corporation, which had to give their approval for the project.

Governor Jay Rockefeller with Mr. Ferguson, Ferguson Construction, who installed Teays tunnel.

A New Hydro Threat Emerges

Dragan was not going to roll over. He hired former, one-term Congressman Mick Staton to convince CSX that the Teays project was unsafe and would create liability for the railroad

Teays Landing Inc. was an independent corporation established by the four outfitters, solely for purposes of establishing an access point on the river for the partners and other outfitters who contracted with them for a New River takeout.

West Virginia outfitters knew how to play in the big leagues and recognized early on that the project faced stiff challenges. They hired former Governor Arch Moore, who practiced law in Charleston, as a consultant primarily to gain influence with CSX. He was still "the Governor" to those who addressed him, and he was running for a third term in 1984. David Arnold and Imre Szylagyi visited Moore in his office and asked him for a rough estimate of the costs. Moore told them if they had to ask that question, they were in the wrong office.

The final decision to approve the project at CSX was dependent on John Snow, Senior Vice President of Operations at CSX. Snow would later be confirmed as 73rd Secretary of the Treasury for President George W. Bush. Despite Dragan's lobbying, the Teays group felt the project was headed for approval. They were so confident; the massive tunnel had already been delivered to the site even before CSX had signed off on the project.

Then the unthinkable happened.

THE WHITEWATER WARS

Dave Arnold was in a state Whitewater Advisory Board meeting in Charleston when he was handed a note from a secretary in the Department of Natural Resources that CSX had killed the Teays project. His heart sank. Within a few minutes, another note was delivered that the project had been approved. He asked the Chairman for a recess and called Arch Moore.

"Governor, what's going on with the Teays project?" Arnold asked. Moore explained that Snow had called him to let him know that CSX was not going to approve the project. Moore said he told Snow, "That's CSX 1, Arch Moore 0." Within minutes Snow called back and reversed his decision. The Teays project was approved.

Arch Moore was first elected governor in 1968 and served two terms to 1977, defeating Jay Rockefeller to win re-election in 1972. He was seriously injured in a helicopter crash days before the 1968 election, declaring publicly that God had voted for him by allowing him to survive. He would be re-elected governor in November 1984 after the Teays decision. The prospect of his re-election probably influenced the CSX turnaround on the Teays' decision.

Moore had always been controversial but had the political and legal skills to overcome charges of corruption until 1990. Federal investigators told him they had caught him on tape discussing how to obstruct the investigation into illegal payments from lobbyists during his election campaign. He pled guilty, but would later try unsuccessfully to withdraw the plea, eventually serving 2 years and 8 months in a federal prison. The Teays group was never involved in this scheme, although some of the alleged illegal activities occurred during this time.

Fortunately, our efforts to save the Gauley River were never drawn into fracas between Teays Landing, Inc. and Dragan. I had to maintain complete impartiality among the outfitters without favoring one clique over the other. It was not easy. After the Teays project was completed, Dragan moved on and it was never mentioned.

Seeds Get Planted

The Gauley issue made other contributions to the future of whitewater recreation that would play out as the years passed, including one of the most consequential pieces of legislation in industry history.

In the spring of 1984 Pope Barrow, our board member and legislative counsel's office in the U.S. House of Representatives, learned about an upcoming hearing in the House Subcommittee on Energy Conservation and Power to discuss bills to amend the Federal Power Act. One version of the legislation would maintain existing preferences to municipalities in the relicensing of hydro projects. Considering the Noah project, Pope asked me if I wanted to testify at the hearing, something I had never done. I jumped at the opportunity.

Pope filled me in on the issues revolving around the legislative proposals. Environmentalists wanted us to support the bill that gave preference to municipalities in the competition for hydropower license applications filed with the Federal Energy Regulatory Commission. They argued we would be more likely to get favorable water releases from local governments. I was skeptical. Instead, I wrote my testimony to propose that projects be required to provide benefits for recreation regardless of who won the license. At the end of the day, municipalities lost their preference for licenses, which had been granted to them in the 1920 Federal Power Act, so we would have sacrificed our interests by tying our benefits to that wagon.

I was a little nervous when it was time to testify. Pope forgot to tell me until we were sitting in the hearing that I would have five minutes to summarize my testimony, so with no time to practice I had to highlight the most important points.

My oral remarks provoked a frown from the recorder as I spoke rapidly and she struggled to keep up. The main point was this: "I am calling for stronger commitment to the recreational values of this nation's waterways than is currently offered by the legislation before you today." Projects were being proposed on seven of the thirteen major whitewater rafting rivers in the East with the potential loss of the economic benefits of whitewater recreation, I said. In 1984 not many people respected the economic potential of whitewater recreation. Remarkably, the testimony was welcomed by the Representatives at the hearing. One of the staff members for the Congressman conducting the hearing was a kayaker who had secured my spot at Pope's request. She was still wearing a cast on her leg from a paddling accident.

I offered a suggested amendment to the legislation that Pope and I wrote during a recess. "In the case of any project which utilizes the hydroelectric potential of any river, and there exists a significant potential for recreational usage, including canoe and whitewater boating which may be affected by the operation of such projects – any license issued for that project shall contain specific conditions considered with the public interests for the enhancement of such recreational usage, including the provision of suitable flows at appropriate times." Of course, the final legislative language was nothing like this, but a seed was planted, and the right people were there to ensure its growth. The final testimony was included in the 800-page hearing record.

In 1986 the Electric Consumers Protection Act (ECPA) passed Congress as the first revision to the Federal Power Act since 1920. It gave immense new power to FERC to set license conditions to include equal protection for fish, wildlife, and recreational values.

U.S.Legal.com describes the bill this way: "The statute also broadened the commission's authority to protect the recreational uses of the nation's rivers, fish and wildlife, and other environmental values. The ECPA requires the Federal Energy Regulatory Commission to give equal consideration to the purposes of energy conservation and protection; mitigation of damages; enhancement of fish and wildlife the protection of recreational opportunities; and the preservation of other aspects of environmental quality while issuing license."

The ramifications for the future of whitewater recreation were immense. In the late eighties Pope and others would help reconstitute American Whitewater (AW) into a major force in hydro power relicensing using the provisions in ECPA to enhance recreational flows at

Seeds Get Planted

FERC licensed projects. AW had been around as a small national, private boater organization for years. With an infusion of energy from some of the same brain trust behind the Gauley River, it grew into a powerful and influential organization expanding whitewater recreation opportunities primarily through participation in FERC hydropower relicensing procedures. With more than 1,900 hydro projects on the books, all of which would have to be relicensed at some point, the recreational potential was immense.

The Corps Surrenders

As fate would have it, in 1984 I proposed to Robin at the Tiki Garden in Beckley with my courage fortified by a couple of Suffering Bastards, their signature drink. The diamond was small, but it was all I could afford on a whitewater warrior's salary. We would tie the knot at an outdoor wedding in October at Carnifex Ferry State Park overlooking Pillow Rock Rapids.

That year the Gauley River Festival reached its peak under CFGR. The Gauley's following was at an all-time high among paddlers, who flocked to it in droves for the Fall drawdown. To promote the event popular whitewater cartoonist William Nealy designed the infamous poster with the Corps turning on the valve to the dam while paddlers ran around like Lilliputians. It was his best work in my opinion.

The Festival had moved to Mountain River Tours campground. About 2,000 paddlers and rafters were on hand. The main act was the debut of "Women in Rubber", which the female paddlers of the Bluegrass Wildwater Association had offered to perform. It was about 9:30 when they took the stage, half a dozen attractive women in swimsuits with a pile of rubber at their feet. At their side was a goofy looking, bespectacled guy wearing

English riding pants and Joffre boots. He was nervously flipping a riding crop. Pope was standing next to me. "This is going too far", he said. These were assertive women and it was their idea, so I figured it was unlikely to go off the rails too much.

Everyone was watching with rapt anticipation as the goofy guy started playing burlesque music from a record player. Over the course of five minutes, the women performed a comedic, reverse strip tease as they slinked into their wetsuits while their sound man slapped his riding boots with his crop. That was it, but it was the signature event of the festival.

One of the planners from the Corps of Engineers showed up for a brief talk. He was giving a hint of something that we were not anticipating, but he was so nervous it was hard to make sense of it. Plus, it just sounded like 'bureaucratese' while we were breathlessly awaiting the Women in Rubber who were next up.

Gauley River Festival poster by William Nealy

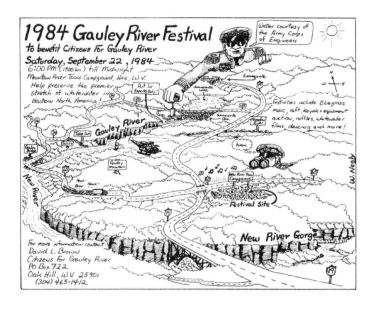

That hint of something would come that Fall when Don Herndon from the Corps called my office a few weeks later. By then I had an office in the Oak Hill Holiday Inn. Don said, "David, I want to drop by your office to bring you our Environmental Impact Statement which proposes to provide reliable releases for whitewater recreation on the Gauley River."

Gauley River Festival poster by William Nealy

Honestly, I could not believe this stunning development. But that changed after he dropped by and gave me a run down and two thick documents which comprised the EIS proposing water releases, a development no one anticipated. The arrogance I had experienced earlier had evaporated. Somebody in the chain of command must have read his team the Riot Act. The Corps was proposing to manage flows following Steve Taylor's operational proposals to provide a 21-day release schedule. There would be a comment period and a public hearing before a final decision.

The Corps must have been quietly working on these voluminous proposals since shortly after our meeting with Gianelli. During the subsequent hearings, there was some minor carping from lake users, but upon conclusion of the comment period, the Corps issued a Record of Decision that allowed them to manage flows to enhance the reliability of the Fall rafting season.

The Corps also withdrew their proposals for the long tunnel project citing a lack of proponents, not to mention opposition from the Congressional delegation led by Congressman Rahall. In a remarkable turnaround in less than two years, the Corps' plans for a hydro project had been vanquished and replaced with reliable water releases for whitewater recreation. That success can be attributed to Gauley's status, Congressman Rahall and the talent pool of paddlers who participated in the effort -- the outfitters and the private boaters who joined forces to save the river.

Preserving the Gauley River Canyon

I left West Virginia in 1985, moving to Knoxville, Tennessee to run a community festival. In October 1986, Congressman Rahall's legislation to make whitewater recreation an official purpose of the Summersville Dam and specify water releases during the Fall drawdown passed Congress. The future of downstream whitewater recreation on the Gauley River was sealed.

In the Water Resource Development Act of 1988, Rahall also made downstream recreation a purpose of 11 Corps projects in the mid-Atlantic region, including dams on the Lehigh and Youghiogheny River in Pennsylvania. I was working for eastern outfitters and had maintained contact with Congressman Rahall's legislative director Jim Zoia. He called me about the bill and I asked him to add a few key Corps projects to the list. This legislation along with a change in attitude within the Corps ushered in an unprecedented era of cooperation from the agency that would eventually lead to improved whitewater recreation activities at the Francis E. Walter project on the Lehigh River and other rivers.

Over the years the Corps made special efforts to ensure the viability of the Gauley season. The Corps of Engineers began to embrace downstream recreation as one of the major benefits of their projects.

David Arnold described the positive outcome from Congressman Rahall's legislative efforts this way, "while we all knew, making whitewater as a project purpose of Summersville Dam would usher in a much more reliable Gauley season, none of us in the industry really understood the impact it would have. Our original concerns were conservation of water in dry years by pulsing during the day. While that was a huge benefit, the Corps also became partners in helping the rafting industry survive and prosper in a state that desperately needed economic diversification. They worked with us in drought and in times of high water. When we had flooding, they reverse pulsed blowing excess whitewater out at night to provide enough storage to keep the water from being too high for rafting during the day. There were very little costs to these operations, but significant economic benefits to the region."

Arnold says the best example of the Corps' cooperation was shortly after September 11, 2001, when America was mostly locked down. "We had been planning the World Rafting Championship for many months prior to September. What would we do? The Corps was an amazing partner in helping us pull off 'The World's' in style. That week, just a few days after nine-eleven, we showed the world what Wild and Wonderful West Virginia really meant. We were the first international event after nine-eleven in America and they helped make it happen."

Congressman Rahall also wanted to preserve the Gauley's canyon through legislation by adding it to the National Park Service's New River Gorge National River. In 1985 I met Pope and Zoia in a motorhome in the parking lot of the Oak Hill Holiday Inn. They were considering a Wild and Scenic River designation. For the outfitters, this designation would be too restrictive. A quarter mile set back is required if the river is designated "Wild". Outfitters owned property along the river. I suggested a National Recreation Area. No matter what the designation, the National Park Service was going to make preservation a priority.

The outfitters wanted to support Congressman Rahall after all his good work on behalf of the river and industry, but there was an additional catch. The National Park Service policy required them to competitively issue a limited number of contracts for commercial services at their units. Outfitters would have to submit bids for those contracts every 10 years after the river was designated and turned over to the National Park Service, essentially requiring the outfitters to bid for the rights to operate their long-established businesses. To avoid this outcome, the legislation included a provision which authorized the National Park Service to allow the West Virginia Department of Natural Resources to continue managing commercial whitewater rafting on the New and Gauley Rivers.

Preserving the Gauley River Canyon

In 1987 the West Virginia National Interest River Conservation Act passed Congress. Along with protecting the Gauley, the Bluestone and the lower Meadow, the bill provided for West Virginia DNR's continued management of commercial rafting in both NPS units on the New and Gauley River. No one else in Congress other than Rahall and Zoia could have pulled that off. It has never been done since. Later Pope sent me a framed copy of the bill signed by Ronald Reagan which was stolen when I moved my office.

The future of the Gauley was secure. There was still work to be done to protect the watershed, but the major battle was over.

American Whitewater's heavy lifting was about to begin as Pope and others looked for an organization through which to pursue similar victories. AW would crank up in the 1990's in time to lead the way during the relicensing of hundreds of hydro projects under ECPA. After Rich Bowers' tenure at AW, Mark Singleton, who once worked for the Nantahala Outdoor Center, took the reins, and led the organization to another level. Mark had attended the very first Gauley Festival at the Burnwood Campground in 1983. AW took over the Gauley River Festival and continues to manage it as the world's number one river festival.

In 1991, outfitters from the east and west joined forces to form a national outfitter organization, America Outdoors. The first President was J.T. Lemons, one of the leading Ocoee outfitters and a good friend. I was working for a plastic company and jumped at the opportunity to apply

THE WHITEWATER WARS

to be AO's Executive Director. I worked for AO for the next 27 years until my retirement at the end of 2018.

The whitewater rafting industry peaked in Central West Virginia in 1995 boosted by Meryl Streep's movie, <u>The River Wild</u>. At one point in the early years, there were thirty outfitters operating in Central West Virginia. By the 1990's about sixteen outfitters were running most of the raft trips on the New and Gauley River. In 1995 160,698 rafting customers were counted on the New River and 65,438 customers on the Gauley River. By 2017 the New was down to 88,000 customers and the Gauley saw 20,231 rafters, a decline of over 55% for those two rivers. The number of outfitters shrank to eight with just four outfitters running over 90% of the trips on the two rivers.

The Catamount project at the base of Summersville Dam began operation in July 2001 with a plate capacity of 80 megawatts. Although the powerhouse had no impact on the watershed, it eliminated one of the most dramatic put-ins for a river trip in the United States. Prior to the project's construction, 2,800 cubic feet per second of water thundered from the penstocks 50 to 60 yards into a pool at the base of the dam. Some customers swore that the ground shook. Mist rose over the dam. Customers paddled out into a vicious eddy line while the roar from the raging torrent behind them drowned out their guides frantic instructions to "paddle hard". It was a baptism that rafters on the Gauley remembered for the rest of their lives.

Preserving the Gauley River Canyon

Demand for rafting has always been driven by word-of-mouth stories about the experience. Dave Arnold thinks the loss of the Gauley's put-in spectacle eliminated one of the trip's most memorable stories.

Rafting's decline in Central West Virginia began in 1997. Successful outfitters diversified and established adventure resorts. The heyday for the whitewater industry in central West Virginia made a significant contribution to preserving the outstanding natural beauty of the Gauley River and lives on today. Ironically, rafting, and other outdoor experiences saw a remarkable resurgence during the coronavirus pandemic of 2020.

The Gauley put in before completion of the Cantamount project, which installed a powerhouse where the penstocks were located. Whitewater Photography, Fayetteville, WV

The Pioneers Move On

Jon Dragan died suddenly on February 12, 2005 after a cerebral hemorrhage. He would be one of the first of a long line of industry founders to fade away. He had sold off his land to the National Park Service around 1990 and his rafting business to his brother Chris. Dragan ran his business with military discipline and vision. It seemed that selling to the National Park Service was always his retirement plan. The location of his property was essential to operation of the New River Gorge National River, which had been designated as a National Park Service unit in 1978. They had to have it. His offices were ideally situated to house Park maintenance vehicles and rangers. His trucks and equipment were painted in a perfect match, Park Service green. His wooden signs were all neatly routered. All NPS had to do was walk in and hang up their logo. They were likely glad to have him out of their hair.

As if it was part of his plan, Jon never made friends with the local NPS staff, referring to them as "toads" while firing off letters critical of their management decisions. They knew where they stood with him too. During an annual volleyball tournament, Jim Carrico, the Park Service Superintendent for New River, named his team,

Carrico's Toads. The motto on their tee shirt was "We Hop to It". NPS would gladly pay to have him removed from their daily lives. Senator Byrd was Chairman of the Senate Appropriations Committee and money was flowing into West Virginia's Park Service units. Dragan just had to pull the levers one more time.

Upon his passing, NPR did a brief eulogy about him and his pioneering outfitting business. The piece closed with one of Jon's favorite expressions, "If you ain't the lead dog, the scenery never changes." That was Dragan's approach to life. If he could not be the lead dog, he was not going to be part of the pack.

Dragan made important contributions to the conservation of West Virginia rivers that few will ever know. One of the greatest of all was providing access to the New River for boaters for 20 years before the National Park Service acquired his property at Fayette Station and holding the land in its natural state until it was sold to the National Park Service.

Another industry pioneer David Arnold and his wife Peggy lived in a tent the first year Class VI opened in 1978. Their story always made me feel better about having to live out of my car for a month. Soon after that first year, he bought the location for their headquarters on the rim of the New River Gorge. It would eventually flower into a resort with a $1 million dollar swimming pool. Their business was founded on quality and style that endured as others faded away. No one in the industry was better at the political game than Dave Arnold. Like

Marc Hunt on the Ocoee, Dave was an indispensable player in the Gauley battle. David is retired but still lives in the house he and Peggy bought years ago just down the road from Class VI's headquarters.

Dave's partners, Jeff and Doug Proctor eventually retired too. Kevin Whelan, one of the original partners, opted out of the company in the 1980's. Doug bought a Selway River rafting company and moved to Stanley, Idaho. Frank Lukacs, who owned North American River Runners until he sold to one of his competitors, is still working, now for Prime Insurance in Utah. Paul Breuer sold Mountain River Tours to Adventures on the Gorge but continued to run his cabin rental business. Imre Szilagyi sold Appalachian Wildwater and retired to Preston County, West Virginia.

Charlie Walbridge and I maintained contact every year at the America Outdoors Association convention. I called on him over the years when critical issues arose related to risk management. Jim Zoia and Pope Barrow retired, presumably in the Washington, D.C. area. Steve Taylor still works for NASA and lives in the DC area. Zoia, Pope and Steve were other critically important players in the Gauley battle.

Congressman Rahall lost his seat in the wave election of 2014 after 38 years in Congress. His accomplishments on behalf of rivers were unprecedented. Without his support the Corps might have succeeded with their long-tunnel diversion project and West Virginia rafting industry would not have prospered.

The Pioneers Move On

A couple years after our Ocoee victory, Marc sold his outfitting company to Nantahala Outdoor Center where he went on to play various leadership roles. By the late nineties, he, his wife Cat, and their family had moved to Asheville where Marc went on to successful careers with nonprofits in economic development and land conservation. He served for a time as vice-mayor of the City of Asheville and recently has been helping lead fundraising for a large parks and greenway project along the French Broad River near his home. Marc and I kayaked the Ocoee on my 70th birthday. We do not see one another often, so it was a special day.

J.T. Lemons and Gary and Beth Harper, who were on the Ocoee from the very first days in 1977, are still in business in the Ocoee River area. J.T. still operates Ocoee Outdoors. The Harpers run a successful whitewater supply business, Man of Rubber, from their property near Reliance, Tennessee just over the ridge from the Ocoee.

In 1990 Western River Guides Association (WRGA) and Eastern Professional River Outfitters Association (EPRO) merged to form America Outdoors (AO), a national outfitter association made up of companies operating in 43 states. As fate would have it, J.T. Lemons was elected the first volunteer President of the Board of Directors and hired me to serve as its first Executive Director. I worked at AO for the next 28 years.

When I took over at AO in 1991, about 150 member companies had actually paid dues. By 2000 the organization had grown to over 600 member companies. We survived every panic and downturn for 27 years as AO grew into the leading, national outfitter organization. Robin would work beside me for almost the entire time, managing our tradeshow and communications. Her experience working as a river guide and National Park Service ranger added authenticity and depth to the organization.

The job would take me to National Parks and Forests all over the country and into the halls of Congress where I testified over 20 times on outdoor recreation issues. I spoke on these issues to gatherings of outfitters across the country and often helped them with their local issues.

Many people assumed the job was all about taking trips and having fun, but it was about helping small businesses run by hard-working men and women overcome bureaucratic challenges and deal with the convoluted authorizations that federal agencies require to permit their operation on public lands. I spent more time in meetings at motels in the dead of winter than I did in the backcountry. One of the greatest benefits was meeting the many outfitters who dedicated themselves to introducing the public to this nation's natural wonders while conscientiously protecting those resources. It was a great ride despite the challenges, and I am forever grateful for the opportunity that started humbly in 1980 on the Ocoee River.

For the most part, outfitters are amazingly resilient and magnanimous. It was easy to believe in them and defend

The Pioneers Move On

their contributions to the public and public lands. Few got rich. If they are lucky and they got in early, their real estate becomes their retirement. One joke describes a career in outfitting this way: "How do you make a million dollars in the outfitting business? It's easy, start with $2 million."

Shortly after our 35th wedding anniversary, Robin and I retired to Jefferson County, Tennessee to be near our daughter Hillary, who is a practicing veterinarian. When she was eight years old, she fell in love with horses on a horse pack trip deep into the wilderness of the Bridger Teton National Forest and Yellowstone National Park. I often wondered how many lives were changed for the better on these trips.

After humble beginnings in the whitewater industry 40 years ago, I am still working as a consultant, helping outfitters with challenges that sometimes seem overwhelming.

This book would not be complete without a mention of Robin's dad, whose life was symbolic of the gift his generation gave to baby boomers. Jack Beard was a P-51 fighter pilot during World War II. Flying out of Italy on his last mission of the war, he was strafing a German train behind enemy lines in eastern Europe when a wire strung to catch enemy aircraft wrapped around this cowling. Pulling back on the stick, he got just high enough to bail out, landing in a field in an eastern European country (can't remember which one). A farmer rushed up to him with a pitchfork. Jack said, "I am American." The farmer said, "I know. I worked in coal mines in West Virginia. I take you to the Germans." Immigrant labor was not treated well by the coal barons of that era.

Jack said the farmer was one of the few people he met during the war who knew anything about the area where he had grown up.

Jack lived to a ripe old age, dying in a Veterans Administration hospital at 97. I spent a few of his last days at his bedside, the least I could do for someone who gave so much to us. After he died, we found a card he sent to his mother from the POW camp through the Red Cross. He assured her that he was warm and well-fed, which was a lie since the Germans were struggling to feed themselves at that point in the war. But it was a comfort to her, nonetheless.

Only the lord knows how much we will miss the men and women of our parent's generation whose hard work gave license to our outdoor recreation pursuits and the whitewater recreation industry that flourished after the War. Many of our parents lived a life of deferred gratifications, a life-style trait rejected by baby boomers. They had too many kids to coddle and protect inside the house, so they shooed them outdoors to roam around while they built a wealthy nation. I have often thought that led many of us to pursue adventure in the outdoors.

The battles for the Ocoee and the Gauley rivers were chapters in the emergence and growth of the whitewater recreation industry. We fought powerful government institutions for control of critical resources, while making important contributions to rural economies and the conservation of rivers. Some hydropower consultants would say whitewater paddling was a step backwards, but little do they know. The conservation of the Gauley River and many other rivers were dependent upon those who paddled their waters. Their wild beauty will remain intact for future generations to admire.

A quote from Mahatma Gandhi that I read years ago summarizes the essence of these river wars: "A small body of determined spirits fired by an unquenchable faith in their mission can alter the course of history."

And without these difficult battles in life, there would be no victories to savor or friends to inhabit the memories of living life close to the edge.

The End

About the Author

David L. Brown was Executive Director of America Outdoors Association, the nation's leading outfitter trade association, since shortly after its formation in 1991 until December 2017. He still works as an industry consultant. David has been a representative of various active travel and outfitter organizations since 1980. He headed the efforts to preserve recreation opportunities on the Ocoee River in Tennessee from 1980 to 1983 and the Gauley River in West Virginia from 1983 to 1985. He has testified before Congress many times on recreation policy and public land management issues. David has kayaked, canoed, hiked, and traveled by horse through many of America's National Parks, Forests, and public lands. His longest expedition was a 24-day, 400-mile canoe trip to the Arctic Ocean on the Coppermine River in Northwest Territories. He is a Navy veteran and was awarded the Navy Commendation Medal with a combat insignia for his service as a boat captain on a Strike Assault Boat in the Mekong Delta, Vietnam in 1970.

Made in the USA
Monee, IL
04 September 2021